EUROPE

Paul Guinness

GEOGRAPHY
10-14

Macdonald

A MACDONALD BOOK

© Macdonald & Co (Publishers) Ltd 1987

First published in Great Britain in 1987 by
Macdonald & Co (Publishers) Ltd
London & Sydney

A BPCC plc company

Printed in Great Britain by
Impact Litho

Macdonald & Co (Publishers) Ltd
Greater London House
Hampstead Road
London NW1 7QX

British Library Cataloguing in Publication Data
Guinness, Paul
    Europe. —(Geography 10-14)
    1. Anthropo-geography—Europe
    I. Title   II. Series
    304.2'094   GF540
    ISBN 0-356-11391-4

Acknowledgements

The publishers thank the following for permission to reproduce their photographs and other copyright materials. The numbers refer to pages and L, R, T, B indicate left, right, top and bottom respectively.

ADN-Zentralbild/Berlin DDR 13; Allsport 4 (Bob Martin), 7T; Barnaby's Picture Library 34, 39; BPCC/Aldus Archive 11T; Daily Telegraph Colour Library 9, 12; John Foley, Paris 43; Ford Motor Company 25; French Government Tourist Office 41B; Courtesy of Friends of the Earth 37T; Sally & Richard Greenhill 31; Robert Harding Picture Library 33; The Hutchison Library 17T (Melanie Friend); Image Bank 23 (Roberto Valladares); Courtesy of The Nationalist and Munster Advertiser, Eire 26–7; Norwegian Institute for Air Research/Acid Rain Information Centre, Manchester Polytechnic 37T; Novosti Press Agency 21T; Pralognan-La Vanoise, Office du Tourisme 41T; Punch 7B; Rex Features 5, 11B, 36, 37B, 46; Shell 35T; Frank Spooner Pictures/Gamma 17B, 47; TASS 21B; Topham 19; ZEFA 14, 28–9, 35B, 38, 44

Cover photograph: Frank Spooner Pictures/Gamma

Newspaper extracts: *Soviet Weekly* (17 August 1985) 10; *The Sunday Press, Dublin* (1 December 1985) 26; *The Times* (15 October 1985) 18, (1 August 1985) 30, 31

The publishers would like to thank Dr Arno Peters and Universum-Verlag, München-Solln, for permission to use the Peters' projection for the map of the world depicted in fig 2, page 6.

The artwork illustrations are by Swanston Graphics Limited

The following illustrations are based on information, maps and diagrams from the sources cited: figs 3 and 5, 5, Population Reference Bureau Inc; fig 1, 10, *Economist*, 1 March 1984; fig 2, 14 and fig 4, 15, Press and Information Office of Federal Republic of Germany; fig 2, 16, fig 3, 19, fig 1, 22, fig 5, 27, JRO Kartografische Verlagsgesellschaft mbH; fig 1, 20, fig 2, 21, *Economist*, 20 April 1985; fig 1, 24, Ford Motor Company; fig 2, 24, *Fortune*, 19 August 1985; fig 1, 28 and fig 4, 29, *The New Europe*, G N Minshull, Hodder and Stoughton 1980; fig 3, 29, EEC Publications; fig 1, 30, *SOPEMI Annual Report 1982*, OECD, 1983; fig 1, 32 and fig 2, 33, *Randstad Holland*, Information and Documentation Centre for the Geography of the Netherlands; fig 1, 34 and fig 3, 35, Finnish Embassy; fig 2, 38, *Economist*, 11 June 1983; fig 1, 40, *L'Etat de l'Environment*, Ministère de la Qualité de la Vie, France; fig 3, 47, *Guardian*, 11 September 1986.

GEOGRAPHY 10–14

Series Editor: Richard Kemp
Buckinghamshire County Adviser in Humanities
Formerly Head of Humanities Faculty.
Lord Williams's School, Thame

Europe

Editors: Emma Aron and John Day
Designer: Jerry Watkiss
Picture Research: Suzanne Williams
Production: Ken Holt

Series Consultants:
Barbara Hamnett, Head of Geography,
J.F.S. Comprehensive School, Camden
David Robinson, Headmaster, Blue Coat School, Dudley
Michael Storm, Staff Inspector of Geography, Inner London Education Authority
Michael Weller, Co-ordinator of PGCE Programme, Bulmershe College of Higher Education, Reading
David Wright, Lecturer in Education, University of East Anglia, Norwich

Editorial note

Economic division of the world
Throughout this series the terms **North** and **South** are used to divide the world into its major areas of different economic characteristics. This is in accord with the model proposed in the *Brandt Report*, which is becoming widely adopted. North and South can be broadly equated with the wealthy, technologically advanced countries and the poorer, less technologically advanced countries respectively. They replace such terms as 'developed countries' and 'developing', 'less developed', or 'underdeveloped countries' or Third World – all of which, for a number of reasons, are less than satisfactory. The term North derives from the fact that the countries in this category, with the exception of Australia and New Zealand, lie in the northern hemisphere and north of the tropics.

Glossary
Terms which readers may be meeting for the first time or which have a special meaning in the context of this book are listed in the glossary on page 48. The first time such a term appears it is printed in **bold type** (except in the case of illustrations). Other appropriate terms are also included.

Contents

_What is Europe?

In August 1986, the USSR topped the medals table in the 14th European Athletics Championships held in Stuttgart. All the countries in picture 1 (except Albania) competed in this major sports meeting, which is held every four years. British athletes won eight gold medals. Fatima Whitbread (javelin) not only won a gold medal in her event, but also broke the world record. Athletics is just one of the many ways in which the countries of Europe are brought together.

Europe is part of the world's rich North. Here, the average **standard of living** is much higher than in the countries of the South (picture 5). However, Europe's wealth is not evenly spread. The people of Switzerland and Sweden enjoy just about the highest average incomes in the world, but some of their near neighbours are much further down the wealth league (picture 3). Even in the richest countries some people live in desperate poverty.

There are many other differences, too – for example, in language, religion and politics. These differences have sometimes caused great problems. In no other continent have so many people been killed in warfare. The horrific First and Second World Wars began in Europe, and only later spread elsewhere. Happily, Europe has enjoyed a long period of peace since 1945 – but will it last? The countries of eastern Europe and

those of western Europe are very suspicious of each other. Each side spends huge sums of money on weapons because it fears that it will be attacked by the other side.

Europeans are also concerned about other issues. Never before has unemployment been so high. Many young people wonder if they will ever get a job. The poor condition of housing is another big problem in many countries. It is at its worst in the inner cities. Concern is also growing over the **environment**. We must take more care of it in the future. Pollution of land, sea and air affects us all. Important decisions on these issues are now being made. These decisions will affect the lives of many generations of people yet to be born.

1 The nations of Europe vary greatly in size. The European part of the Soviet Union is the giant of the continent. In comparison, Ireland, Luxembourg and Iceland are very small indeed. Overall, however, Europe is not big. Of the seven continents of the world, only Australia is smaller.

Country	Population	GNP per person 1981 US dollars	Country	Population	GNP per person 1981 US dollars	Country	Population	GNP per person 1981 US dollars
USSR (European part)	222.0	4 701	East Germany	16.7	7 286	Austria	7.6	10 250
West Germany	61.5	13 520	Czechoslovakia	15.4	5 610	Switzerland	6.5	17 150
Italy	56.3	6 830	Netherlands	14.4	11 140	Denmark	5.1	12 790
UK	56.0	8 950	Hungary	10.7	n.a.	Finland	4.8	10 380
France	54.6	12 130	Portugal	9.9	2 534	Norway	4.1	13 800
Spain	38.4	5 770	Greece	9.9	4 540	Ireland	3.5	5 350
Poland	36.6	4 187	Belgium	9.9	11 980	Albania	2.9	n.a.
Yugoslavia	22.8	2 789	Bulgaria	8.9	4 413	Luxembourg	0.4	13 900
Romania	22.7	2 546	Sweden	8.3	14 500	Iceland	0.2	12 550

3 The Gross National Product (GNP) is the wealth created by a country in a year through the production of goods and services. Here, the GNP for each country has been divided by its population. This gives us GNP per person, a measure of the average wealth of people in a country. It is not a perfect measure but it is one of the best available.

4 (above) Terrorism is a growing problem in Europe. It has affected many countries including Ireland, Britain, France, Italy and Spain. This photograph shows the devastation caused by a bomb planted in Bologna by a neo-Fascist group. Most countries now take precautions against terrorism, which seemed unthinkable 20 years ago. Why do terrorists seek to kill and maim people in this way?

World region	GNP per person (US dollars, 1981)
Africa	783
Asia	968
South America	2 063
North America	12 405
Europe	10 025
USSR	4 701
Oceania	8 864
World average	2 754

5 (above) GNP per person by world region. This shows the differences between the rich North and the poor South. Japan, in Asia, is one of the richest countries in the world, while some Asian countries have a GNP per person much lower than $968.

2 (left) Marlise Goehr running in the Women's 4 by 100 metres at the 1986 European Athletics Championships.

1 Copy picture 1. Using an atlas, write in the name of each capital city (shown by the dots).

2 If you won a holiday to any European country, which would you choose? Give your reasons.

3 Copy picture 1. Look at the data for GNP per person.
(a) Shade the countries on your map as follows:

$13 000 and over	Blue
$ 9 000 – 12 999	Brown
$ 5 000 – 8 999	Green
$ 4 999 and below	Yellow

(b) Which parts of Europe are the richest? Which are the poorest?
(c) Is this what you expected?

4 Draw a bar graph to show the gap in GNP per person between regions of the North and South.

5 Project idea:
(a) Ask everyone in the class to make a list of the European countries they have visited. Collect all your results together.
(b) Write a table showing the countries visited most at the top, and those visited least, or not at all, at the bottom.
(c) Show your results on a copy of picture 1.
(d) Try to explain the differences shown in your table.
(e) Make a collection of European coins and drawings of European flags. Display your collection.

‾Not as Big as You Thought?

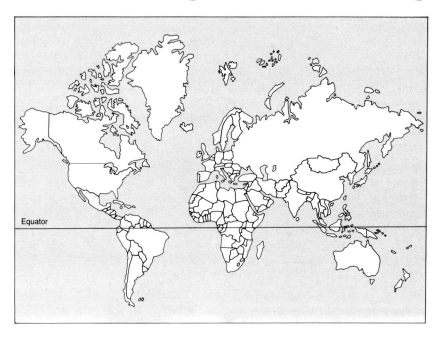

1 (above) The Mercator map projection shows the world like this. Mercator represented the earth as a cylinder on which the lines of longitude were parallel to each other. This made the map easy for navigators to use, but it shows countries which are located closer to the poles than to the equator larger than they really are. The size of North America, Europe, and northern Asia are all magnified. There is much less land south of the Equator, and most of it is far from the South Pole. In this way, the continents of the South are reduced in size.

2 (below) Arno Peters' world map is an equal-area map projection. The area of each continent on the map represents its true area on the globe. The Mercator map shows Europe larger than South America, but you can see from Peters' map that South America is almost double the size of Europe. However, there is a problem. To get equal area, Peters has distorted the shape of the continents. Look at a globe and see this for yourself.

Europe is only a small part of our planet. Yet some maps of the world show it to be much larger than it actually is. We have to look back hundreds of years to discover why.

Some maps used today are based on the world chart drawn by Geradus Mercator in Germany in 1569. At this time, Europeans thought they lived at the centre of civilization. It was an age of discovery as explorers found new lands such as the Americas. Quite wrongly, most Europeans saw themselves as better than the native peoples of these places. They found it hard to understand their achievements and ways of life. This led to mistreatment of other peoples, as European armies took over their lands. This attitude of European superiority is known today as eurocentricity.

It is not surprising, then, that Mercator placed Europe at the centre of his map and exaggerated its size (picture 1). But why are such distorted maps still used now? One reason is that the earth is a sphere. It is, therefore, very difficult to show it accurately on flat paper. Another reason is that, even today, the rich North tends to see itself as more important than the poorer South. All map projections have their faults. Only a globe can show the earth as it really is. Some map-makers have tried to put this right. In 1970, Dr Arno Peters drew a new world map (picture 2). Here the area of each continent on the map reflects its

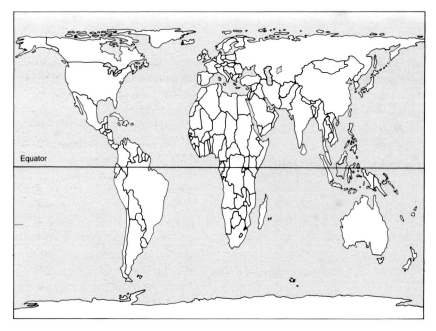

3 This is the image that many Europeans have of the British. How would you feel about being thought of in this way?

4 An example of eurocentricity. The Victorians justified imperialism by portraying all the peoples whom they wished to rule as backward. In this Punch cartoon of 1853, the Chinese are shown as blocking the path to progress.

BARBARIAN DRAGON THAT WILL EAT UP "THE BROTHER OF THE MOON."

true size on the earth. But to do this, Peters distorted the real shape of the continents.

The information we receive from maps and elsewhere (TV, papers and comics, for example) is important. It helps to form our attitudes to and **images** of other people and places. Poor information can result in people forming narrow **stereotyped** views. For example, comedians and cartoonists in Britain often show the Irish as heavy drinkers and not very clever. But the truth is that alcohol consumption in Ireland is lower than in many European countries, and education standards are high. In other European countries, the popular images of the British are the City businessman in pin-striped suit, bowler hat and umbrella, or the football hooligan. Again, very few British people are either of these. What are your images of the Soviet Union, India and Nigeria? Do you think they are correct?

5 (below) The continents vary greatly in size. This can be shown accurately by drawing proportional squares. To do this, you need the square root of each figure in the middle column. These are given in the last column. Each square root is the length of the side of the square for a continent.

Continent	Million square kilometres	Length of side of square in cm (for Question 6)
Asia	44.4	6.7
Africa	30.2	5.5
North America	24.3	4.9
South America	17.8	4.2
Antarctica	14.2	3.8
Europe	10.4	3.2
Australia	7.7	2.8

1 Look at pictures 1 and 2. In what ways are the maps different from each other?

2 Name one advantage and one disadvantage of (a) the Peters' map projection, (b) the Mercator projection.

3 (a) Make a copy of picture 2. Turn it upside down. Now write the name of each continent in the correct place.
(b) There is nothing wrong in showing the world this way. How do you feel about it?

4 Comedians and cartoons often show people from other countries in a way that is very misleading. Write about as many examples of stereotyping as you can.

5 Use a globe or an atlas to find the shortest distance from France to each of the other six continents.

6 (a) On a sheet of graph paper draw seven squares to show how the continents differ in size. Use the measurements given in picture 5.
(b) Think of another way to show the size of the continents on graph paper.
(c) How many times larger than Europe are the continents of (i) North America, (ii) Africa, (iii) Asia?

7 (a) Which foreign country do you know most about?
(b) Explain your choice.
(c) Write a couple of paragraphs to describe the country and its people.

8 Imagine you have a penfriend in another continent. She wants you to tell her more about the country you live in. What would you write?

Urals to Atlantic

Europe has many contrasting natural environments, which have a big influence on its peoples' lives. The continent stretches from the Ural Mountains in the east to the Atlantic Ocean in the west and from the Arctic in the north to the Mediterranean Sea in the south.

Europe is the world's most crowded continent. It has an average of 98 people for every square kilometre. But this average figure hides big differences. Few people live in the very cold and mountainous regions. It is almost impossible to make a living there. **Population density** is also low where soil is poor and in remote, isolated areas. Many more people live in lowland areas with good soils and warmer climates. Coastal areas, too, usually have higher than average population densities. This is partly because they have milder climates than areas much further inland.

The physical environment is not alone in deciding where people live. Other factors are also important. The main one is work. People usually live where they can find jobs. The densely populated areas in picture 3 are the main industrial regions of Europe. Here much wealth is created through the production of goods and services.

Many industrial areas have grown up near important raw materials. Examples are the large coalfields of the Ruhr in West Germany and of Yorkshire, Nottinghamshire and Derbyshire in Britain. Elsewhere, industry has developed in the most easily reached parts of the continent.

1 Europe is the far western part of the huge Eurasian land mass. Eurasia extends from the Atlantic in the west to the Pacific shores of China and the USSR in the east. Most geographers agree that the boundary between Europe and Asia follows important features of the physical landscape. In the east, the two continents are separated by the Ural Mountains and the Ural River. The Caspian Sea and the Caucusus Mountains form the dividing line in the south-east. The Black Sea, the Bosporus, the Sea of Marmara and the Dardanelles form the southern boundary. The Mediterranean Sea separates Europe from Africa.

Look at an atlas to see how many cities are situated on the coast, by major rivers and in lowlands where natural routeways meet. London, Paris and Moscow are all examples of places which are easy to reach from elsewhere.

The distribution of population shown in picture 3 is different to what it was 300 years ago. It will surely change again in the future. People are often on the move. If living standards fall in some places, people may look for a better life elsewhere. In the last 50 years, many people have moved from the north to the south of Britain for this reason.

2 Population densities around the world. (Population density is the number of people living in a square kilometre.)

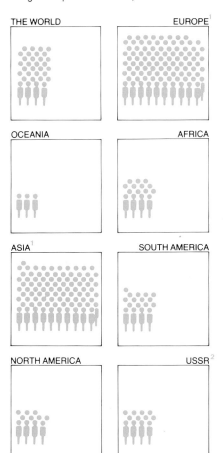

THE WORLD

EUROPE[1]

OCEANIA

AFRICA

ASIA[1]

SOUTH AMERICA

NORTH AMERICA

USSR[2]

☐ = Each box represents a square km

▯ = 1 person/km[2]

[1] = The figures for Europe and Asia do not include the USSR

[2] = USSR is considered separately from Europe. The average shown is a result of higher density in the European part of the USSR and lower density in the Asian part.

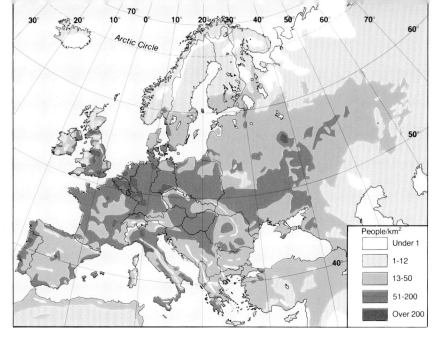

People/km^2

☐	Under 1
	1-12
	13-50
	51-200
	Over 200

1 Look at picture 1. Use an atlas to identify the mountain ranges numbered 1 to 9.

2 The Volga and Danube are Europe's longest rivers. Use an atlas to (a) measure the length of each river, (b) list the countries each river flows through.

3 Look at temperature graphs for Europe in an atlas. Write a paragraph for each of Moscow, London, Oslo and Athens, describing temperature changes throughout the year.

4 Look at picture 3.
(a) Compare the population density between 50°–60° N and 60°–70° N and suggest reasons for the differences.
(b) Name the largest cities in each zone of latitude.

3 The areas where most people live are shown in red. The largest cities are found in these areas. Notice how few people live in the cold northern lands and in mountainous areas.

5 Look at picture 2.
(a) Use the key to find the population density of each world region.
(b) Can you suggest reasons to explain the big differences? Use an atlas to help you.

6 (a) Do you think that the population density is high, medium or low where you live? Give reasons.
(b) Describe other places near you where the population density is different.

4 A photograph of Leningrad and the Gulf of Finland taken from an earth satellite. Can you pick out the places where people live? What can you say about population density?

Superpower Battlefield?

On 14 November 1983, the first Cruise missiles arrived in Britain from the United States. They were flown into the US airforce base at Greenham Common, Berkshire, as part of a NATO plan to site over 400 Cruise missiles in five west European countries (Britain, Italy, West Germany, Belgium and the Netherlands). They are aimed at the Warsaw Pact countries of eastern Europe. Each nuclear missile is four times more powerful than the nuclear bombs which destroyed the Japanese cities of Hiroshima and Nagasaki in 1945 (picture 3).

Many people do not want nuclear weapons in Britain. They think it will make another war more likely. Big demonstrations have been organized by the Campaign for Nuclear Disarmament (CND). It wants the British government to change its mind and send Cruise back to the United States. CND wants all countries which have nuclear weapons to give them up (**multilateral disarmament**). It says Britain should set a good example by being the first to do this (**unilateral disarmament**).

Other people think that Cruise will make us safer. They say that it will make NATO stronger and deter the Warsaw Pact from

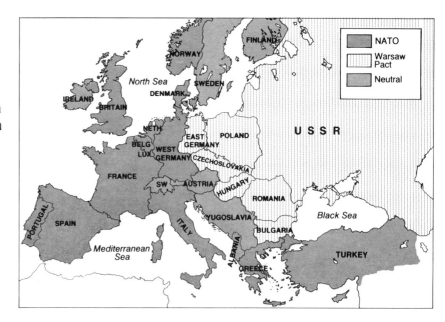

1 The North Atlantic Treaty Organization (NATO) was formed in 1949 to defend the West against a possible attack from the Soviet Union. NATO is made up of the United States, Canada and 13 western and southern European nations. In 1955, the Soviet Union and its allies formed the Warsaw Pact. Both NATO and the Warsaw Pact hold regular military exercises to prepare for attack by the other side.

attacking us. The Warsaw Pact countries have hundreds of nuclear weapons aimed at London, Paris, Rome and many other places in the west.

The United States and the Soviet Union are the **superpowers** of the world. They control most of the nuclear weapons in the west and the east. Every year the stockpile of weapons gets larger

Will I ever get to live in peace?   Drawn by V. UBOREVICH-BOROVSKY

2 A cartoon from the *Soviet Weekly* of 17 August 1985. This is how the Soviet Union sees the siting of American missiles in western Europe. The Soviets claim that it is the United States which is the great threat to world peace. But the Soviet Union has sited hundreds of its own nuclear missiles in eastern European countries such as Czechoslovakia and East Germany. Can you imagine how an American cartoonist might draw the missile situation in Europe?

3 So far, only two nuclear bombs have ever been exploded in war. They were dropped from US bomber aircraft on the cities of Hiroshima (6 August 1945) and Nagasaki (9 August 1945). On 14 August 1945 Japan surrendered and the Second World War came to an end. This photograph shows what happened to Hiroshima.

and larger. There are enough to destroy the world many times over. If the two superpowers fight, then Europe will probably be the main battlefield. From time to time, the two sides talk to each other about reducing the number of missiles. But they find it hard to agree about how this should be done.

Picture 1 shows the boundary between east and west, marked by electric fences and patrolled by armed guards. This is Europe's most recent division. It began in 1945, with the defeat of Germany and its allies at the end of the Second World War. There were other divisions before this.

Not all European countries are in NATO or the Warsaw Pact. Some countries are neutral. They do not take one side or the other. They hope that they will not be involved in any war between east and west.

1 The US and USSR are superpowers. What does this mean?

2 Look at picture 1. Make lists of the countries which are (a) in NATO, (b) in the Warsaw Pact, (c) neutral.

3 Why are some countries neutral? Give as many reasons as you can.

4 (a) Describe picture 3.
(b) Look at a map of Japan.
(i) Which continent is Japan in?
(ii) On which Japanese islands are Hiroshima and Nagasaki?
(iii) How far apart are the two cities?

5 (a) Do you think a nuclear war could ever happen in Europe?
(b) How could Europe be made a safer place to live in?

6 (a) How long is the border between NATO and the Warsaw Pact?
(b) Which national boundaries does it follow?

7 Look at picture 4.
(a) Do you think that this is a reasonable way to protest against something you do not agree with?
(b) In what other ways do people protest against decisions their governments have taken?

4 In September 1981, a group of women camped outside the main gate of the Greenham Common airforce base. Their aim is to get Cruise missiles sent back to the United States. Today there are camps outside all nine gates. They are totally organized and run by women.

East Germany: the Communist Life

Alex and Renata Muller and their children Ingrid and Franz live in Karl-Marx-Stadt. This city of over 300 000 people was once called Chemnitz, but it was renamed in honour of Karl Marx, the first person to write in detail about the idea of **communism**. The Mullers enjoy their lifestyle, but it is very different from life in the west.

The main aim of communism is a society where everybody is equal. Industry and commerce are owned and run by the state so that the benefits are shared by everyone. In the west, the profits of private companies only go to people who own shares in them. The Mullers think the communist way is fairer. But, Alex's cousin Bridgit in West Germany thinks that private companies run business better. She says the west's higher incomes prove this.

1 After Germany was defeated in the Second World War, the USA, USSR, Britain and France occupied its territory. Germany was divided into four occupation zones. The capital city, Berlin, which was deep inside the Soviet zone, was also divided into four areas. In May 1949, West Germany, with the agreement of Britain, France and the USA, became a separate country. In October 1949, East Germany became a new nation.

2 On 13 August 1961 a wall was built by the East Germans dividing East and West Berlin. At the same time, the rest of the frontier between the two countries was closed with high barbed-wire fences and watch-towers. The East German government wanted to stop people leaving the country. Between 1945 and 1961 over four million people left the communist nation. Most went to West Germany. Special permits are needed to travel between the two sides of Berlin.

Renata is a doctor in one of the city's hospitals. Many East German doctors are women. In fact, women do many jobs in communist countries which are mainly done by men in the west. Alex is an engineer in a chemical factory. He is also a trade union official and meets regularly with the factory managers to discuss working conditions and increases in production. There is little open disagreement.

Ingrid and Franz are at secondary school. The school is well equipped. Science, technology and mathematics are important in all schools. East Germany has some of the most modern factories in eastern Europe. Well-qualified people are needed to run them.

Not all East Germans are as happy as the Mullers. Some dislike the government's great control over their lives. Religion is not encouraged. Openly religious people are often discriminated against. For example, they are unlikely to get top jobs. It is very difficult to criticize the government. TV and newspapers usually say what the government wants them to. It is also hard for

East Germans to get permission to travel to the west.

The USSR has great influence over East Germany. Almost 40% of the country's trade is with its giant Warsaw Pact partner. East Germany has agreed to the siting of nuclear missiles on its territory by the USSR. In West Germany, the US has done the same. Relations between East and West Germany are much better now than they once were. They both know that if the superpowers fight, they will be the first to suffer.

3 Karl-Marx-Stadt, named after the founder of modern communism, is a big industrial centre, and a road and rail junction.

4 Women do more highly skilled and highly paid jobs in East Germany than they do in Britain. These are a few examples.

Percentage who are Women		
Occupation	East Germany	Britain
Judges	51	4
MPs	32	4
Doctors	52	18
Dentists	57	18

1 (a) What does picture 3 tell you about Karl-Marx-Stadt?
(b) Why was the city given this name?
(c) How far is the city from the border with West Germany?
(d) List the other large cities in East Germany (picture 1).

2 (a) How big is East Germany compared to West Germany?
(b) How long is the border between the two countries?
(c) Which other countries does East Germany border?

3 (a) Picture 5 compares eastern and western Europe in eight different ways. In which ways do you think (i) eastern Europe is best, (ii) western Europe is best?
(b) What is the main aim of communism?
(c) Do you think you could live happily in a communist country, like the Mullers do? Give reasons for your answer.

4 (a) Draw bar graphs to show the information in picture 4.
(b) List the jobs in Britain which employ few, if any, women.
(c) Do you think more women will be employed in these jobs in the future?

5 (a) Describe the scene in picture 2.
(b) Why was the Berlin Wall built?
(c) Suggest ways in which the Wall has affected the people of Berlin.

6 **Project idea:** Find out all you can about Karl Marx. He is a very famous person and you will get plenty of information from your local library. What do you think of his ideas?

WESTERN EUROPE		EASTERN EUROPE
Mainly privately owned. Some large industries may be state run.	 Industry	Owned by the state. Very small businesses may be privately owned.
Many different parties contest elections. New governments can bring great change.	Government	No opposition parties. At elections there is a single list of official communist party candidates. Less likelihood of great change.
A growing problem. Very high in the older industrial areas.	Unemployment	Very little. Everyone has the right to a job.
Completely separate from management. Sometimes great disagreement leading to strikes.	Trades Unions	Work more closely with management to achieve higher production. Strikes are very rare.
Complete religious freedom.	Religion	Communism is officially opposed to religion but many people are deeply religious.
Privately-owned shops. Wide variety of goods from all over the world.	Shopping	Large stores are state-owned. Small shops can be privately owned. Usually a smaller choice of goods, mainly from eastern Europe. Shortages can occur.
Generally good but can vary greatly within one country and between countries.	Services	Generally good – seen as a high priority. Emphasis tends to be on health, education and transport.
Great choice, if people can afford it.	Holidays	Most people not allowed to leave the east. Lower incomes also restrict choice.

5 These are some of the major differences between east and west.

West Germany: Another Way of Life

Bridgit and Hans Schuster and their only child Eva live in West Berlin. Bridgit was born in East Berlin but moved across the city with her parents in 1958. This was three years before the Wall was built. The total population of East and West Berlin is 3.2 million. It is the largest city in the two countries.

Like the Schusters, many European families today are small. In the past, families were larger. The small family is a particular worry for West Berlin. Because the city is isolated from the rest of West Germany, many young people have left. The result is that 23% of West Berliners are over 65, compared with 15% in West Germany as a whole.

West Germany is like the other nations of western Europe. It is called a **democracy**. According to one dictionary, this is

'government by the people or their elected representatives'. At elections, there is a choice of parties. Each party wants to run the country in a different way. If a new party is elected to government, many changes can

1 This shows the Kufürstendamm, West Berlin's busy shopping area. In the background is the Kaiser Wilhelm Memorial Church.

occur in a short space of time. People are often very critical of what the government does. They can say what they think more freely than in East Germany. Of course, the government does have power, but individuals are not so closely controlled by it.

Like the Mullers, the Schusters enjoy a good lifestyle. Hans is a manager with an engineering firm. Bridgit is a secretary with an electronics company. Last year, however, Hans thought he

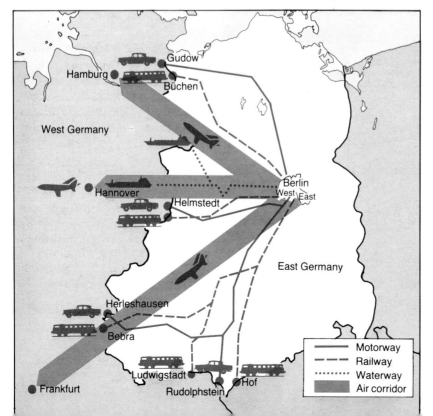

2 This is how West Berlin keeps in contact with the rest of West Germany. In 1948 the USSR blocked all the land and water routes to West Germany from Berlin. Everything had to be flown in. It was a mammoth task. The blockade was withdrawn in 1949. But, understandably, West Berliners feel isolated from the rest of West Germany.

might lose his job. His firm cut its workforce by over 200 people. Fortunately, Hans was not included. Unemployment is lower than in most west European countries but it is still a great problem. Over two million West Germans were out of work in 1984. The Schusters may earn more money than the Mullers, but the Mullers have more secure jobs.

West Germany is one of the world's leading industrial nations. The government runs some industries such as the electricity supply, telephones and the railways. Most industry, however, is privately owned. You have probably heard of some of the most famous names shown in picture 4.

Measurement	East Germany	West Germany
GNP per person ($)	7 286	13 520
Cars per 1000 people	180	384
Telephones per 1000 people	176	404
TV sets per 1000 people	342	337
Daily amount of food per person (calories)	3 746	3 537
Number of people per room	1.1	1.5
Children dying under the age of 1 year	12 in 1000 births	12 in 1000 births

3 East and West Germany are among the world's top ten industrial nations. Average incomes are much higher in West Germany, but, using other measurements, East Germany comes out better.

4 The main industrial regions of West Germany. Many world famous companies have factories there.

1 (a) What is a democracy?
(b) Why do most people in the west believe that communist governments are not democratic?

2 Why do you think that European families today are smaller than they used to be?

3 (a) Why is West Berlin's population older than West Germany's national average?
(b) Is this seen as a problem?

4 (a) Describe the transport links between West Berlin and the rest of West Germany.
(b) Why are they so important?

5 (a) Make a copy of picture 4. With the help of an atlas name the 22 industrial cities shown by the factory symbols.
(b) List the products made by as many of the companies named as you can.

6 Look at picture 3.
(a) Which of the seven measurements (i) favour West Germany, (ii) favour East Germany?
(b) Which measurements do you think are the most important?
(c) List three other ways in which the two countries might be compared.

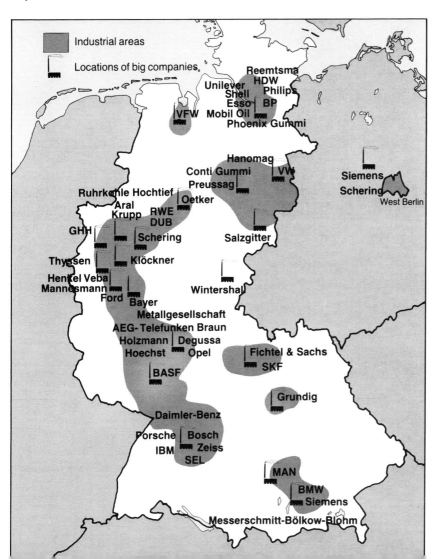

15

The European Community

From 1991, all new cars in Britain will have to use lead-free petrol. This will help to give cleaner air.

This decision was not made in Parliament in London. It was taken in Strasbourg, the Parliament of the European Economic Community (EEC). The EEC is having an increasing influence on the lives of its 325 million people. It affects the way we work and play, the food we eat and the air we breath.

The EEC was formed in 1957 when France, West Germany, Italy, the Netherlands, Belgium and Luxembourg signed the Treaty of Rome. Britain, Denmark and Ireland joined in 1973 and Greece in 1981. Spain and Portugal became members in 1986.

The Community arose from a wish to form a peaceful and prosperous Europe after the terrible experience of two World Wars. It was thought that another war would be less likely to happen if countries were bound together by strong economic and social links. The first major task was to form a Common Market. This meant the free movement of trade, workers and investment between the member countries.

Before the Common Market, each country used to charge taxes, known as tariffs, on

3 A comparison of the EEC with the rest of the world.

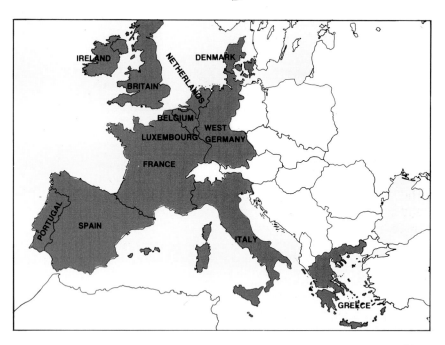

1 (above) The 12 member countries of the EEC.

2 (below) There are big differences in living standards between EEC members.

Country	GNP per person 1983 US dollars	Unemployment rate 1984-85 %	Cars per 1000 people, 1984	TV per 1000 people, 1981	Telephones per 1000 people, 1982
Denmark	10 980	10.3	272	365	705
W Germany	10 680	8.5	402	355	510
France	9 500	10.5	378	350	540
Netherlands	9 320	15.7	330	310	560
Belgium	8 230	13.3	332	300	400
Luxembourg	8 000	1.5	332	250	550
Great Britain	7 980	11.8	300	360	520
Italy	6 275	10.5	345	260	380
Ireland	5 060	15.7	203	200	225
Spain	4 200	20.0	220	200	330
Greece	3 715	8.0	108	155	310
Portugal	2 050	11.5	108	140	155

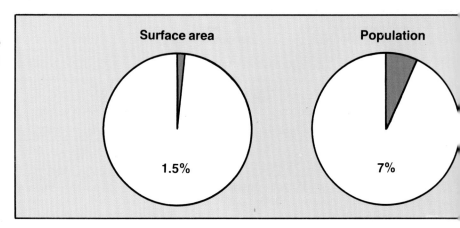

imported goods. These tariffs have been removed between members. EEC countries now charge the same tariffs on goods from elsewhere in the world. This has led to much greater trade between the members. EEC citizens can look for jobs in any member country. Many British workers have been attracted to West Germany where there are more jobs available.

The EEC produces more goods and services than any other **trade bloc** or single country in the world. The 12 countries have more influence together than they would apart. On many matters of world importance, they have a common policy. However, as the EEC has become

larger, more problems have arisen. Some of these will be very difficult to solve. Yet the member countries are gradually coming closer together. In the year 2000 will we see ourselves as Europeans first, rather than as Britons, Italians or Germans...?

4 The European Parliament discusses EEC affairs in Strasbourg. The Community's administrative HQ, shown on the cover, is in Brussels.

1 (a) Draw a time chart to show how the EEC has grown since 1957.
(b) Calculate the EEC's population each time new countries joined (see picture 3, page 5).
(c) Which are the four largest countries in population?

2 (a) Why was the EEC formed?
(b) Not everyone in Britain was happy when the country joined the EEC. Can you think of any reasons why? Ask some adults what they thought then. Do they feel the same way now?

3 (a) In which country is the headquarters of the EEC?
(b) Do you think this is a good place for the EEC countries to meet. Give reasons for your answer.

4 Look at picture 2.
(a) Draw a bar graph to show per capita GNP for the 12 countries.
(b) Where do the three most recent members rank on your graph?
(c) Are these countries in the same positions for the other measurements?

5 Look at picture 3. Work out the EEC's share of world trade and GNP using a protractor.

6 Imagine you want to visit the capital cities of all the EEC countries. Plan your route to fly the least possible distance. Start and finish in London.

7 **Project idea:** Look through your newspapers for a week. Cut out anything about the EEC. Make a class display.

5 These demonstrators are protesting in Strasbourg against EEC agricultural policy.

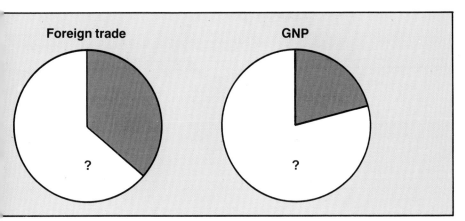

Foreign trade

?

GNP

?

Butter Mountains and Wine Lakes

The Common Agricultural Policy (CAP) has caused more argument within the EEC than any other issue. Some countries get lots of money from it, while others pay the bill. Two-thirds of the entire EEC budget is spent on the CAP. Britain, in particular, thinks much of this money could be used in better ways.

The CAP was set up in 1957 by Article 39 of the Treaty of Rome. It had clear aims that most people agreed with (picture 2).

CAP 'a blot on Europe's landscape'

By John Young, Agricultural Correspondent

The EEC common agricultural policy was a blot on Europe's economic, social and political landscape, Mr Michael Montague, chairman of the National Consumer Council, said last night.

Mr Montague condemned the CAP as bad for consumers, bad for taxpayers, bad for farmers, bad for industry, bad for Europe's relations with the rest of the world and even bad for Europe.

This year the butter "mountain" had exceeded a million tonnes, equivalent to 4 billion packs. Stocks of skimmed milk powder were more than 500,000 tonnes, most of which would be fed, with subsidies, back to cows to produce more surplus milk.

The beef mountain was now 750,000 tonnes, enough to make 16 billion beefburgers. In spite of the relatively bad harvest this year, about 10 million extra tonnes of grain would go into storage to join last year's 22 million tonne surplus.

Last year more than 5,000 unsold oranges, 5,000 lemons and 40 cauliflowers were destroyed every minute, he said.

The cost of supporting Europe's farmers, who were 7.6 per cent of its population, was estimated to add more than £7 a week to an average family's food bill.

1 (above) The Common Agricultural Policy has many critics. This extract is from the *Times*, 15 October 1985.

2 (right) These are the aims of the CAP as stated by the Treaty of Rome 1957.

Today, however, the EEC produces much more food and wine than it needs. Some of the surplus is sold abroad, but much is still left over. This is stored in warehouses throughout the EEC. Yet food is still destroyed, because there is not enough room for it all, while thousands of Africans die every day because of lack of food. Many people think the EEC should do more to help starving people in countries such as Ethiopia and Sudan.

Farming was very different when the EEC began. Farms were smaller, more people worked on the land and much less food was produced. In fact, a lot of food had to be imported from other parts of the world.

Most CAP money has been spent on **guaranteed prices**. The EEC promises to buy what the farmer grows at a price set in advance. If the farmer can get a higher price in the open market, all well and good. But if food prices on the open market are low, farmers can rely on getting EEC guaranteed prices. These apply to a wide range of foods. They are usually generous and higher than farmers get elsewhere in the world. For example, in 1979 the guaranteed price for butter was four times higher than the lowest price on the world markets. Because of the good prices, EEC farmers have produced more each year.

Britain wants these guaranteed prices reduced. This would cut the food surplus and leave more money for other needs such as industry. Other countries want to keep high prices. They say that the farmers need such protection.

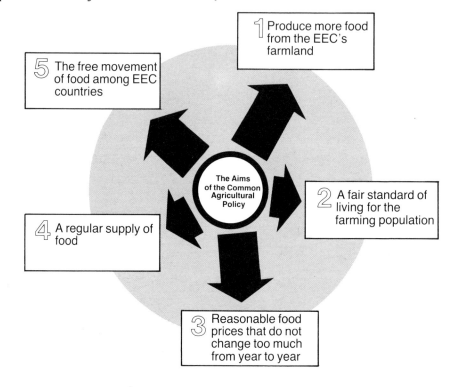

1 Produce more food from the EEC's farmland

2 A fair standard of living for the farming population

3 Reasonable food prices that do not change too much from year to year

4 A regular supply of food

5 The free movement of food among EEC countries

The Aims of the Common Agricultural Policy

3 There are big differences in the amounts of food produced by each of the countries of the EEC. France and Italy together account for 45% of the value of farm products in the EEC.

CAP money has also been spent on farm modernization. Machinery has replaced much animal and human labour and the use of fertilizers and pesticides has increased greatly. Many farms have been made into compact units. Better pensions have encouraged older farmers to retire – this gives opportunities to young farmers with new ideas.

Such changes have had a big effect on the environment. Hedgerows and their wildlife have vanished as fields have been made larger. Farm chemicals pollute rivers. There are problems getting rid of animal waste from large livestock farms. Progress always has costs as well as benefits.

4 Higher farm production has had a big effect on the landscape. Fields have been combined by tearing up hedgerows. In many areas the animals and flowers that lived in them have gone forever.

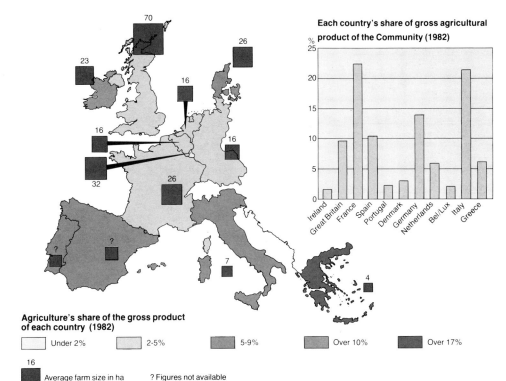

Each country's share of gross agricultural product of the Community (1982)

Agriculture's share of the gross product of each country (1982)

| Under 2% | 2-5% | 5-9% | Over 10% | Over 17% |

16 Average farm size in ha   ? Figures not available

1 What do you think about the aims of the CAP?

2 Look at picture 1. Write a fact list which shows how big the overproduction of food is in the EEC.

3 (a) What are guaranteed prices?
(b) How do they encourage higher food production?
(c) The EEC countries often find it very difficult to agree on the level of guaranteed prices. Suggest why.
(d) What do you think would happen if these guaranteed prices were greatly reduced by the EEC?

4 The EEC is often criticized for over-producing food when millions are starving elsewhere in the world. What are your views on this?

5 In what ways has higher food output affected the environment?

6 Look at picture 3.
(a) Write a table ranking the 12 nations in order of average farm size.

(b) In which countries does agriculture account for over 5% of gross product?
(c) Which countries contribute at least 10% to the EEC's gross agricultural product?

7 (a) Describe how farming has changed in the EEC over the last 30 years?
(b) Do you think that all these changes have been for the best?

8 Visit your local supermarket. How much of the variety of food and drink comes from (a) the EEC, (b) other parts of the world?

Comecon

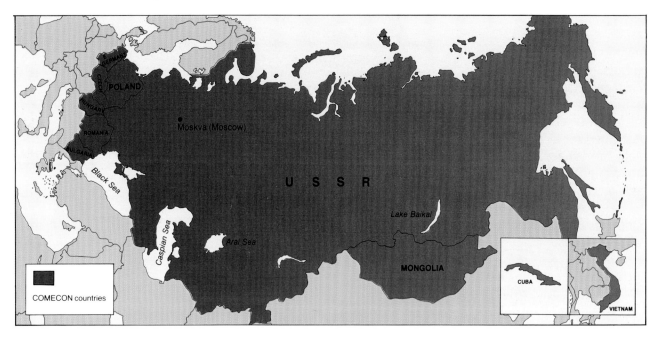

Eastern Europe's answer to the EEC is Comecon – the Council for Mutual Economic Assistance. It began in 1949 when the USSR, Bulgaria, Czechoslovakia, Hungary, Poland and Romania agreed to increase economic cooperation. These countries were soon joined by Albania and East Germany. However, unlike the EEC, Comecon has spread outside Europe. Mongolia (1962), Cuba (1972), and Vietnam (1978) are now also members of Comecon.

The aims of Comecon are:

(a) To encourage economic and technical advance.
(b) To close the gap between its richer and poorer nations.
(c) To strengthen its ability to defend itself.

Comecon sees specialization as an important way of improving the standard of living. This means that each country concentrates on the industries it runs best. Among other industries, East Germany specializes in optical equipment, Czechoslovakia in nuclear reactors and Bulgaria in electronics. However, specialization has not gone as far as it was once hoped. It has not been easy to get agreement amongst Comecon's members. No country wants to be completely left out of important industries.

Comecon is dominated by the Soviet Union. It is by far the largest member country, both in population and in the volume of its trade (picture 2). There is a clear pattern in the exchange of goods and services between the countries. In general, the Soviet Union exports raw materials. In return, it gets manufactured goods from the rest of eastern Europe. The other member countries rely heavily on large

1 Comecon has member countries in three continents. Albania has taken no part in Comecon since 1961, but has not officially left. The Comecon countries are often said to have 'centrally planned economies'. This means that government controls almost all the industry and commerce. Note that this map uses a different projection from those on page 6.

imports of oil and gas from the Soviet Union. The price of this energy is much lower than the world market price. This is of great benefit to the smaller east European countries. But it gives the Soviet Union great economical and political power over its neighbours.

The Comecon countries have cooperated on a number of very large projects, sharing the cost and the benefits. The biggest scheme was the 2750 km long Soyuz gas pipeline. Completed in 1978, it carries 15 000 million cubic metres of Soviet natural gas to the other east European countries each year.

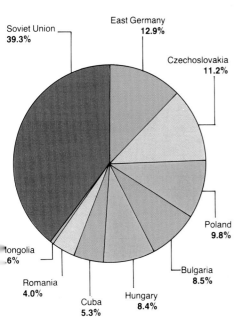

East Germany
12.9%

Soviet Union
39.3%

Czechoslovakia
11.2%

Poland
9.8%

Bulgaria
8.5%

Hungary
8.4%

Cuba
5.3%

Romania
4.0%

Mongolia
.6%

2 (left) Percentage share of trade amongst the Comecon countries in 1983. The Soviet Union dominates this trade.

4 (below) Large, modern container lorries like these carry goods between the member countries of Comecon.

3 The Soyuz gas pipeline is one of several large projects costing millions of pounds that the Comecon nations have built together. The word 'Soyuz' means 'union' in English.

Comecon has important links with other parts of the world. There has been a great increase in trade with the developing nations of the South. Contact with western Europe is also growing. For example, the Italian car firm Fiat has helped to develop the car industry in eastern Europe. In 1983 a gas pipeline was built to transfer natural gas to western Europe. More trade in the future between eastern and western Europe might make war between NATO and the Warsaw Pact less likely.

1 (a) How many countries are in Comecon?
(b) Which were the original member countries?
(c) In which continent is each country?

2 (a) Look at an atlas or globe to find the capital cities of Cuba, Mongolia and Vietnam.
(b) How far is each capital city from Moscow?

3 (a) Why was Comecon formed?
(b) State one way in which Comecon is different from the EEC.

4 (a) What is 'specialization'?
(b) What are its main advantage and main disadvantage?

5 Look at picture 2.
(a) Why does the Soviet Union have such a big share of Comecon trade?
(b) What is the combined share of the other east European countries?
(c) Suggest three reasons which might explain why Mongolia's share is so small.

6 Describe one of the large projects completed through cooperation between the Comecon countries.

7 The EEC has, at times, cut its food mountain by selling produce to Comecon at much lower prices than we pay for it. What do you think about this trade? Should it continue?

8 **Project idea:** Comecon countries have invested much money in their car industries in recent years. Find out the names of those cars which are on sale in Britain. How do they compare in price to cars which are made in western Europe? What do you think of the east European cars?

Changing Patterns of Work

Monique Blanc lives in Lyon, France's second largest city. She works as a computer programmer with the giant Hewlett-Packard company. Like Monique, 70% of Lyon's workforce are employed in the **service industries** (also known as tertiary industries). The rest of the workforce are employed in the **manufacturing industries** (also known as secondary industries). They make goods such as clothes, machines, furniture and food products. Monique has not always lived in the city. She was born on a farm near the small town of Villefranche, 32 km north-west of Lyon. In 1970, the Blancs decided to sell up. The farm was small and, even with CAP guaranteed prices, only gave a low income. Better paid jobs could be had in the city. The

move broke a centuries-old family tradition of farming. Mr Blanc is now a machine operator in a chemical factory. His wife works as a machinist for a clothing firm.

Work and working conditions have changed a great deal in France in the last 20 years. Big changes have occurred even since 1970 (picture 1). The mechanization of farming, mining, forestry and fishing means that fewer people now work in these industries (called **primary industries**). Many primary jobs are in the countryside. Secondary and tertiary jobs, however, are mainly in towns. So, employment has become even more concentrated in towns such as Lyon.

In the most technically advanced

countries, the number of jobs in manufacturing is also falling. Automation is replacing human labour. In some factories, robots do **assembly line** jobs that once employed thousands of workers. Automation is costly to install. But it saves money for firms in the long run, because the wage bill can be cut drastically. Automation is also safer and it can always be relied on to produce high-quality work quickly.

What has happened to the people who have lost jobs in factories? Some have found work

1 Since 1970 there have been big changes in the number of jobs and types of work available. The pattern of change is similar for all the EEC countries. For example, more people are now finding work in the service industries.

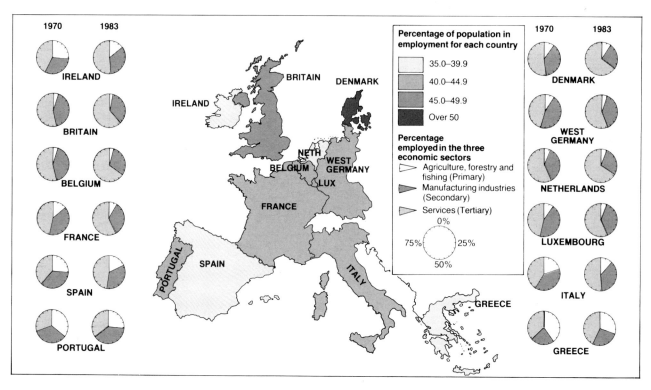

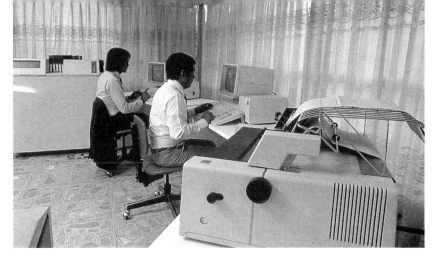

2 (above) Banks, building societies, insurance companies and similar offices are increasingly relying on computers to speed up work and do more business. Fewer new office jobs will therefore be created.

3 (below) Triangular graph for question 5. The employment structures of Britain and Greece are already plotted. From the pie charts in picture 1 you can see that in Britain 5% of the workforce is in primary, 30% in secondary and 65% in tertiary industry. In Greece it is very different. There is 29% in primary, 28% in secondary and 43% in tertiary industry.

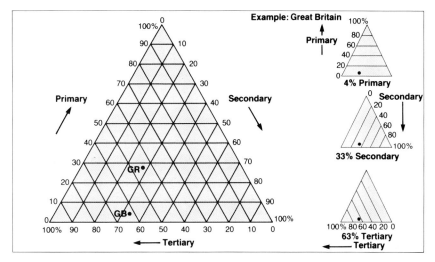

in the tertiary sector. Others have been less fortunate – they are unemployed. In most of the countries of western Europe, the number of people out of work is higher than ever before. But this is not the end of the story. Tertiary employment is also undergoing great change. Here too, automation is replacing people. Public transport jobs have gone with the introduction of automatic ticket machines and one-person operated buses and trains. In post offices, machines are increasingly used to sort mail. In banks and insurance companies, there are fewer new jobs because of the use of word processors and computers. Few jobs have been unaffected by automation. In the past, most people spent their working lives doing the same type of job. In the future, people may have to retrain throughout their lives for new jobs. The pace of change is faster than ever before.

1 Look at picture 1.
(a) Which four countries have the highest percentage employment in (i) primary industries, (ii) the service industries?
(b) Calculate the average GNP per person for each of these two groups of countries (page 16).

2 (a) Suggest reasons why employment in the primary industries has fallen in all countries since 1970.
(b) Name four jobs in each of the primary, secondary and tertiary industries.

3 (a) Why did the Blanc family move from Villefranche to Lyon?
(b) How do you think Monique's parents felt about leaving the farm?

4 Look at an atlas map of France.

(a) How far is Lyon from Paris and Marseilles?
(b) Which two rivers join at Lyon?
(c) Write down the route you would take if you were driving from Calais to Lyon. Draw a map to show the towns you would go through.

5 Complete the triangular graph to show the 1983 employment structure for all 12 EEC nations.

6 (a) Draw a pie chart to show what you think Africa's employment structure is.
(b) Why have you drawn it this way?

7 (a) Make a list of the different jobs done in your school.
(b) Could any of them be automated? How might this be done?

Multinational Companies

The Ford Motor Company is a huge, worldwide business. It employs almost 400 000 people in more than 100 countries. Its headquarters are in Dearborn in the state of Michigan, USA. This is where it all began when Henry Ford built his first car in 1896. The company was formed in 1903. Ford grew rapidly, and its first assembly plant outside North America was set up in Britain in 1911. From here it spread around the world.

In Europe, Ford produces over 1.5 million cars, commercial vehicles and tractors a year. This takes place in 28 manufacturing and assembly centres in seven countries. Altogether, 100 000 Europeans work for this giant **multinational company**.

Ford's decision to build cars in Europe was welcomed by most people. Many jobs have been created. Companies such as glass and lamp manufacturers also benefit from the work Ford gives them. Many cars made in Britain are sold abroad, helping the **balance of payments**.

However, multinationals are not popular with everyone. Trade unions are concerned about the way production and **investment** can be quickly moved from one country to another. Companies might do this because of the cost of labour. Spain has become very popular with some of the world's big car makers because wages there are much lower than in most European countries. Changes might also occur

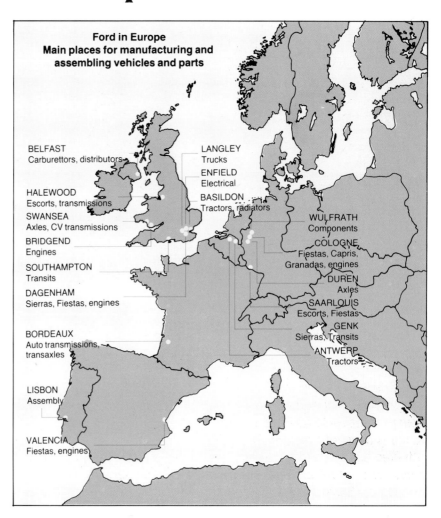

Ford in Europe
Main places for manufacturing and assembling vehicles and parts

BELFAST
Carburettors, distributors

HALEWOOD
Escorts, transmissions

SWANSEA
Axles, CV transmissions

BRIDGEND
Engines

SOUTHAMPTON
Transits

DAGENHAM
Sierras, Fiestas, engines

BORDEAUX
Auto transmissions, transaxles

LISBON
Assembly

VALENCIA
Fiestas, engines

LANGLEY
Trucks

ENFIELD
Electrical

BASILDON
Tractors, radiators

WULFRATH
Components

COLOGNE
Fiestas, Capris, Granadas, engines

DUREN
Axles

SAARLOUIS
Escorts, Fiestas

GENK
Sierras, Transits

ANTWERP
Tractors

because of the time it takes to make a car in a particular country. For example, British carmakers are said to be slower than German and Japanese. At the huge Dagenham works, east of London, the workforce has been cut from 25 000 in 1978 to 13 000 in 1985, as Ford have used more automation and cut the cost of wages.

Ford is now building many more cars in the countries of the South. Wages here are much lower than in Europe and there is little trade union organization. Also, car sales are rising rapidly

1 Outside Europe Ford has manufacturing plants in the United States, Argentina, Australia, Brazil, Canada, the Philippines, Mexico, South Africa, Taiwan and Venezuela. There are assembly plants in Malaysia, New Zealand, Singapore, South Korea and Thailand. In addition, there are sales and distribution centres in many other countries.

in parts of the South. This is a big worry for the European factories. Whole cars are now rarely built in one country. Different parts are made wherever production is cheapest. These are then sent to the Ford network around the world for assembly. We are in the age of the 'world car' which can be made almost anywhere.

2 This is the Ford factory at Cologne, where Fiestas, Capris and Granadas are built. It is their main factory in West Germany. Ford has a workforce of more than 36 000 in the country.

3 (right) Nearly 2500 robots in Ford plants around the world weld and paint car bodies and do other manufacturing jobs. There are 500 in Britain. Robots speed up production, but reduce the number of jobs for people.

Governments are also concerned about the great power of the multinationals. If Ford decided to leave Britain, it would not only be disastrous for the areas around the factories. It would also be a great blow to the country's economy. However, the government could do little about it. Many peoples' lives could be affected by decisions made far away in a boardroom in Dearborn, Michigan.

1 (a) On a world outline map, label all the countries where Ford manufacturing and assembly takes place. (See picture 1 and caption.)
(b) Make a note of the make of the nearest 50 cars to your school.
(i) How many are Ford cars?
(ii) Which companies made the others?

2 (a) What is a multinational company?
(b) Which European countries do not have multinational companies?

3 In the last 20 years multinational companies owned in the North have opened 25 000 factories in the countries of the South. Why has this happened?

4 Why is Ford investing so much money in robots?

5 Look at picture 4.
(a) On an outline map of the world, label the headquarters of the world's 20 largest industrial corporations.
(b) How many are in each continent?
(c) How many have you heard of?
(d) Draw a graph to show the 1984 sales of the top five companies.

Rank 1984	Company	Headquarters	Industry	Sales $000
1	Exxon	New York	Petroleum refining	90 854 000
2	Royal Dutch/Shell Group	The Hague/London	Petroleum refining	84 864 598
3	General Motors	Detroit	Motor vehicles & parts	83 889 900
4	Mobil	New York	Petroleum refining	56 047 000
5	Ford Motor	Dearborn, Mich.	Motor vehicles & parts	52 366 400
6	British Petroleum	London	Petroleum refining	50 662 063
7	Texaco	Harrison, NY	Petroleum refining	47 334 000
8	International Business Machines	Armonk, NY	Off. equip., computers	45 937 000
9	E.I. du Pont de Nemours	Wilmington, Del.	Chemicals	35 915 000
10	American Tel. & Tel.	New York	Electronics, appliances	33 187 500
11	General Electric	Fairfield, Conn.	Electronics, appliances	27 947 000
12	Standard Oil (Ind.)	Chicago	Petroleum refining	26 949 000
13	Chevron	San Francisco	Petroleum refining	26 798 000
14	ENI	Rome	Petroleum refining	25 798 221
15	Atlantic Richfield	Los Angeles	Petroleum refining	24 686 000
16	Toyota Motor	Toyota City	Motor vehicles & parts	24 110 656
17	IRI	Rome	Metal manufacturing	23 353 993
18	Unilever	London/Rotterdam	Food	21 598 000
19	Shell Oil	Houston	Petroleum refining	20 701 000
20	Elf-Aquitaine	Paris	Petroleum refining	20 662 330

4 The 20 largest industrial corporations in the world in 1984. They are ranked by the value of products sold.

High Unemployment – Here to Stay?

The Republic of Ireland has one of the highest unemployment levels in Europe. In 1984, one in every six people was out of work. In parts of the country it is much worse. Nearly half the men in the town of Carrick-on-Suir are without a job (picture 2). Some young people have gone to Dublin, Cork and Limerick to look for work. But unemployment is high in the cities too. Other young people have emigrated to Britain and the United States. Most of them did not want to go. It is hard to leave family and friends.

Emigration is not new to Ireland. The population is only just over half what it was in the 1830s. The shortage of work during the

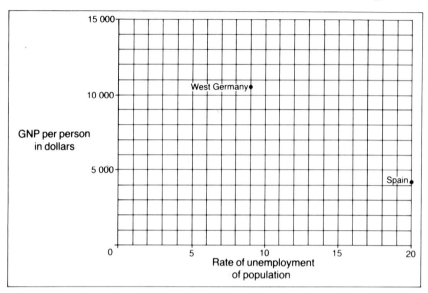

1 This scattergraph shows unemployment and GNP per person for two EEC countries. See question 1 (a).

2 This extract is from an Irish national newspaper, *The Sunday Press*, 1 December 1985.

last 150 years has left many people with little choice but to go abroad. The economy improved in the 1970s, and more people moved into Ireland than left it. But the good times did not last long.

Carrick-on-Suir is not the town it used to be. Derelict factories still bear the names of companies that people once worked for. Shops have been hit hard. Fewer wage packets mean less money to spend, and some shops have had to close.

The government tries to bring foreign companies to Ireland. New factories often get big grants and tax benefits. But, other countries compete with

Six members out of work

By Michael Bance

The members of Carrick-on-Suir Urban Council debate a question of unemployment with more authority than most – six of the nine councillors are on the dole. With male unemployment now a staggering 42% in the South Tipperary town, party politics are abandoned when the councillors put their heads together in an attempt to come up with ideas to bring their home town out of the depression.

The bottom fell out of the local economy when the Carrick Tannery closed, with the collapse of Irish Leathers, and an ultra-modern aerospace industry, Rexnord, suddenly shut shop in the same week as it was announced that it was expanding its workforce of 60 to 250.

The out-of-work councillors are using their free time to organise deputations to Government Ministers, and to the leader of the opposition, and are hopeful that things may look up in the New Year.

Councillor Jimmy Hogan, with over 33 years employed as a machine operator in the tannery, took voluntary redundancy when the industry went into a minor decline in 1983. Councillor Jack Lawlor with 35 years in the same industry, was a group purchasing manager with the tannery when it collapsed; Councillor Dennis Bourke, was a clerk in Clover Meats in Waterford, where he was employed for 16 years up to its closure last Christmas; Councillor Pat Ryan was a construction worker, but due to the slump in building has not worked for two years and as he is over 40 sees little prospects of picking up a job; Councillor Sheamus Fogarty lives at Faugheen, outside Carrick, and he joined the dole queue when he sold his vegetable shop in the town. And even the Council chairman, Liam Dwyer, is among the ranks of the idle.

Liam, also a former tannery worker, gave up his factory job eight years ago, to become a full time singer. But even the cabaret scene has taken a hammering locally and he now finds himself without a regular income.

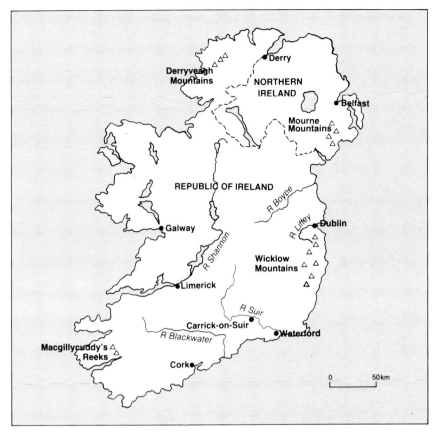

3 The town of Carrick-on-Suir is situated on the banks of one of Ireland's main rivers, the Suir. It is in County Tipperary.

Ireland by offering similar **incentives**. So some companies only stay in Ireland for a short time. They make the most of government grants and then leave for elsewhere. It is hard to attract the largest foreign companies. The country lacks raw materials and has only a small population and few industries to buy goods. Also, goods for export have to go by sea. This increases costs.

The government is particularly worried by youth unemployment. Like most other European countries, Ireland has youth training schemes. This gives young people work experience. It teaches skills that will help in working life. But youth training only lasts a short time. Ireland now has a serious drugs problem. Juvenile crime is rising fast. Both are at their worst in Dublin, the capital city. It is not certain why this is so, but many people think high unemployment is a major reason.

4 (right) Rising unemployment is a serious problem in all EEC countries. This bar chart shows the figures for 1984–85.

5 (left) These protesters were employees of the tannery in Carrick-on-Suir. Several industries in Carrick-on-Suir have packed up since the early 1980s, with many jobs lost and factories left to decay. See picture 2.

1 (a) Complete the scattergraph by plotting unemployment (picture 4) against GNP per person (page 16) for the other 10 EEC countries.
(b) Do all the richest countries have the lowest unemployment rates?

2 Look at picture 3.
(a) How far is Carrick-on-Suir from Cork, Dublin and Limerick?
(b) In which direction is each city from Carrick-on-Suir?
(c) Why have some young people left the town for Britain and the United States?
(d) How would you feel if you had to go a long way from home to find work?

3 (a) What jobs did each of the six unemployed councillors once do? (See picture 2.)
(b) Draw a labelled diagram to show why some of the shops in the town have closed.

4 (a) List any businesses near your school which have closed in recent years.
(b) Have any new ones opened?
(c) How high is unemployment in the area?
(d) Look at your local newspaper. Make a list of the types of jobs which are advertised.

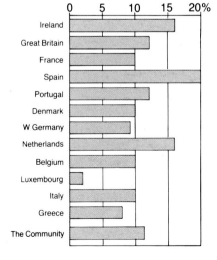

The Mezzogiorno – Problem Region

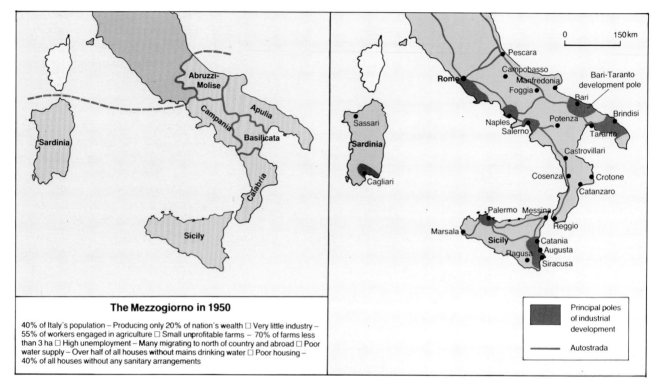

The Mezzogiorno in 1950

40% of Italy's population – Producing only 20% of nation's wealth □ Very little industry – 55% of workers engaged in agriculture □ Small unprofitable farms – 70% of farms less than 3 ha □ High unemployment – Many migrating to north of country and abroad □ Poor water supply – Over half of all houses without mains drinking water □ Poor housing – 40% of all houses without any sanitary arrangements

Principal poles of industrial development

Autostrada

'Il Mezzogiorno' – the land of the noon-day sun – is the name given by Italians to their country's southern provinces. The rugged landscape and picturesque towns of the area are popular with tourists. But this hot, dry and hilly region is one of the poorest parts of western Europe. For centuries, the standard of living has been well below that of the northern provinces. Because of the difference in living standards and wealth between the north and the south, Italy has sometimes been called a land of two nations.

The Mezzogiorno's problems are partly due to its landscape and climate. Over 40% of the land is too steep or remote for farming. There is a shortage of water. Many parts of the south have only 500 mm of rain a year. (The average rainfall in the south of England is about 700 mm a year.) This makes life difficult. History has also played its part. For so long, Italy's wealth has been concentrated in the north in cities such as Milan, Florence, Turin, Venice and in Rome. There has been very little investment in the south, where most people lived in the countryside.

Conditions became so bad that something had to be done (picture 1). In March 1950, the government set up The Fund for the South. Its first job was to improve farming. This was done in two ways. First, a lot of farmland lay in large estates of over 200 ha, called 'latifundi'. Most were very inefficient. They were often owned by people who lived in the north and rarely visited them. The government

1 The map on the left shows the seven provinces of the Mezzogiorno. The Fund for the South spent its money on industry in a number of growth poles shown in the map on the right. The new autostradas (motorways) have also been very important in helping industry to grow. The markets of northern Italy and the rest of Europe can now be reached more easily, quickly and cheaply.

2 Life in this beautiful landscape of the Mezzogiorno can be harsh, and there is still much poverty, despite the Italian government's efforts to improve conditions and create jobs.

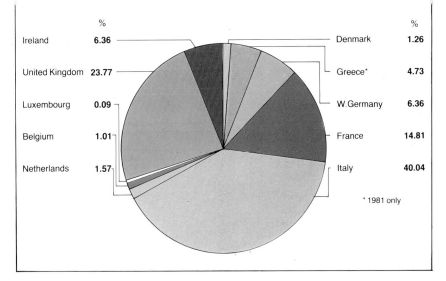

	%			%
Ireland	6.36		Denmark	1.26
United Kingdom	23.77		Greece*	4.73
Luxembourg	0.09		W.Germany	6.36
Belgium	1.01		France	14.81
Netherlands	1.57		Italy	40.04

* 1981 only

3 The EEC has a Regional Development Fund to help the Community's poorest regions. From 1975 to 1981 Italy has gained more from the Fund than any other country. This money has been spent in the Mezzogiorno.

took over many of the latifundi and divided them into small farms. These were given to people who had no land. Secondly, modern farming methods were encouraged. Tractors began to replace horses, more fertilizer was used and swampland was drained.

General living conditions were also improved. Schools, hospitals and training centres were built. Mains water supply was brought to hundreds of small towns and villages. Telephone systems were installed, and road and railway links improved. From the late 1950s more money was invested in industry in areas called 'growth poles'. It was hoped that prosperity would spread out from the growth poles to the rest of the Mezzogiorno.

Has the plan worked? Yes – but not as well as the government once hoped. Wages are now closer to those in the north, but there is still a considerable gap. Many more people are employed in industry, but deserted factories show that not all investment has succeeded. However, the overall quality of life is much better. All countries have their problem regions. Most, like Italy, try to do something about it.

1 (a) Draw a table with two columns. In one, name the seven provinces of the Mezzogiorno. In the other, list the main cities in each province.
(b) How far from Naples is (i) Palermo, (ii) Brindisi, (iii) Cagliari?

2 (a) On an outline map of the Mezzogiorno shade in the land over 400 m high. (Use an atlas.)
(b) How much of the region is above the 400 m level?
(c) What is the name of the major mountain range.
(d) What problems can so much high land cause?

3 (a) In an atlas find climate graphs for two places in Italy – one north and one south. Describe the differences in temperature and rainfall.
(b) Why is the climate in the south more difficult for farming?
(c) Suggest one way that farmers can overcome the climatic conditions.

4 (a) What was the standard of living like in the Mezzogiorno in 1950?
(b) How have conditions changed since then?
(c) What do you think are the four most important measures of the quality of life in a region?

5 (a) Where are the growth poles in the Mezzogiorno?
(b) What is their purpose?
(c) Use an atlas to explain the routes followed by the autostradas.

6 Which countries received most money from the European Regional Development Fund between 1975 and 1981? Suggest why.

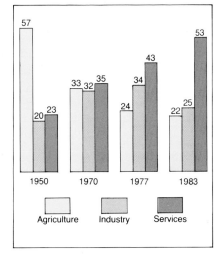

4 How people have moved from one kind of work to another since the Fund for the South was set up in 1950.

29

The miracle workers that Germany no longer wants

AT 4.45 one morning, on a street corner in the ill-famed Reperbahn district of Hamburg, Semra Bilir, a 24-year-old Turkish girl, poured petrol over her body and lit it, in protest against the "Ausländer-feindlichkeit" – hostility against foreigners – of the Germans. She died, leaving behind her "guest-worker" parents, three sisters, and 361 poems.

Her last poem, written the morning of her death, on May 28, 1982, describes what it is like to live, despised and taunted in the Turkish ghettos of Germany. It ends with the words "... the Germans say, if you don't like it, get out; go back to Turkey." ["Turken Raus" – "Turks Out" – a distrubing reminder of the Nazi party cry of the 1930s "Juden Raus", is scrawled on walls all over West German cities.]

Under a new federal government law, a payment of DM 10,500 (£2,840), plus DM 1,500 per child, has been on offer to any foreign worker who, unemployed through redundancy, or over the past six months continuously in part-time work, had registered before yesterday his willingness to leave the country permanently and depart within 30 days of registration. Everybody knows the law is aimed at the Turks alone: EEC nationals are free to work in any EEC country, and workers from Spain, Yugoslavia, Italy and Portugal have in general adapted and been accepted by the Germans.

Workers from	Receiving countries							
	Austria	Belgium	France	Germany thousands	Lux	Neth	Sweden	Switz
Algeria		3.2	382.1			0.2		
Austria				87.0				19.5
Finland				3.0			104.4	
Greece		10.7		132.2		2.3	7.3	4.9
Italy	2.1	90.5	157.6	316.1	9.2	10.5		234.9
Morocco		37.3	171.9			40.2		
Portugal		6.2	434.6	57.1	15.9	5.6		9.3
Spain	0.2	32.0	128.9	85.9	1.0	12.7		63.4
Tunisia		4.7	73.2			1.5		
Turkey	30.4	23.0		637.1		59.5		22.7
Yugoslavia	113.9	3.1		357.7	0.7	8.4	23.0	34.3
Other EEC	12.5	81.5	49.4	151.6	23.4	45.5	39.5	85.2
Non-EEC	17.2	40.0	194.2	254.2	2.0	52.1	59.3	40.9
Total	176.3	332.2	1 591.1	2 081.9	52.2	238.5	233.5	515.1

1 The age of the migrant worker began in the 1950s. The richer countries of western Europe did not have enough people to fill all the available jobs. In the poorer countries there were too few jobs.

2 (left) Anti-Turkish feeling in West Germany, taken from a report in the *Times*.

From 1950 to the mid-1970s over two million foreign workers moved to West Germany. They came mainly from southern Europe. At that time, the booming German economy had more jobs than German workers to fill them. These **guestworkers** took the unskilled and 'dirty' jobs that most Germans no longer wanted. But times have changed. West Germany now has over two million unemployed and is trying to persuade many of its foreign workers to return home. Work is scarce and desperate Germans are prepared to take lower paid jobs.

There are 1.5 million Turks in West Germany – 560 000 workers and their families, They form the largest **minority** group in the country. Most are in low paid city-based jobs. They live mainly in poor inner city areas where housing is deteriorating and overcrowded. Such a slum area, where many people from one minority group live, is called a **ghetto**. Because of their appearance and way of life, the Turks are seen as more 'foreign' than guestworkers from Yugoslavia, Spain, Italy and Portugal. They are the foreigners West Germans most want to leave (picture 2). **Neo-Nazi** groups have made violent attacks on the Turkish community. When times are hard, minority groups are often made the scapegoats for a country's economic and social problems.

Other countries in northern and western Europe also welcomed foreign workers at the same time as West Germany. In Britain many came from the West Indies, while over 300 000 Algerians went to France in search of work. However, these last two groups are different from the Turkish guestworkers – they have been entitled to settle permanently. The reason for this lies in the history of these countries. From 1500, for about 400 years, a number of European countries (particularly Britain, France, Spain, Portugal, Germany and the Netherlands) **colonized** much of the world outside Europe. They used their armies to take over other lands for two main reasons. They wanted the wealth of their minerals, farms and forests and they needed these countries for military reasons.

20 attacks in 'wave of racist violence'

By Pat Healy, Race Relations Correspondent

More than 20 serious assaults were recorded in the first half of July in what a monitoring group in east London described yesterday as evidence of growing racist violence against black people.

The Tower Hamlets Community Alliance for Police Accountability (CAPA) said the assaults included a man who needed 13 stitches for a head wound after being attacked by three white youths using metal bars: a boy aged 12 being slashed in the back while walking along a school corridor.

Three days before the arson attack on the Kassam family of Ilford, which resulted in the deaths of Mrs Shamira Kassam and her three children, a Bengali family in Bethnal Green suffered a similar attack, CAPA says in its latest bulletin.

The Bethnal Green family, identified only as the Ali family, escaped unhurt.

CAPA accuses the police and other authorities of indifference and insensitivity to the plight of black families and claims that "death is the natural conclusion of the tolerance of systematic racist harassment". Its bulletin says that between 1976 and 1981 31 black people were murdered by racists.

The Metropolitan Police said yesterday that they were not aware of the attack on the Ali family, and were no nearer to arresting anyone for the Kassam family deaths. But 40 officers were involved in the investigation. 1,500 people had been interviewed and between 300 and 400 statements taken.

Today, however, nearly all the old European colonies are independent. But they often keep strong links with their old rulers. A number of the islands in the West Indies were British ruled. It is not surprising, then, that in the 1950s and 1960s some British companies advertised in West Indian newspapers to fill job vacancies. Many West Indians eagerly took up these offers of secure work. Without this **immigration**, big industries such as the National Health Service and the transport services could not have been run so well.

3 In Britain 4% of the population is black. Blacks are often discriminated against by the white majority because of the colour of their skin and their different culture. At times, such **racism** can result in terrible violence.

4 The Turks have the lowest standard of living in West Germany. They mainly live in the worst inner-city housing.

1 (a) Why are there so many migrant workers in north-west Europe?
(b) When did most of them arrive?
(c) Why are so many of them no longer needed?

2 (a) Why is life more difficult for the Turks than for other minority groups in West Germany?
(b) How do you feel about the newspaper report in picture 2?

3 (a) Which three countries employ most guestworkers?
(b) From which three countries do most migrant workers come?

4 (a) Why do people of the same nationality tend to group together when they go to live in another country?
(b) Describe the conditions you would expect to find in a ghetto.
(c) Make a list of the jobs you would expect migrant workers to do in West Germany.

5 Look in an encyclopaedia for a map of Africa in the early 1900s, showing European colonization.
(a) Which countries had colonies?
(b) Rank them in order of the amount of land area they ruled.
(c) Try to find out when the larger African countries gained their independence.

6 Look at picture 3.
(a) What do you think of this report from the *Times*?
(b) Suggest reasons why the police are finding it difficult to stop this racial violence.

7 (a) Are there pupils and teachers from minority groups in your school?
(b) Do you think they are sometimes treated unfairly because the majority group sees them as being different?

The Randstad: People and Space

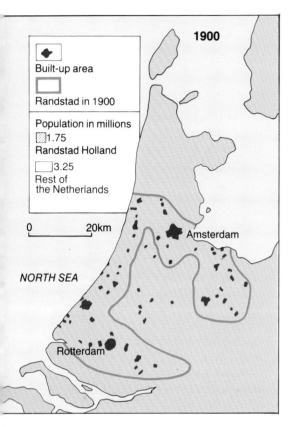

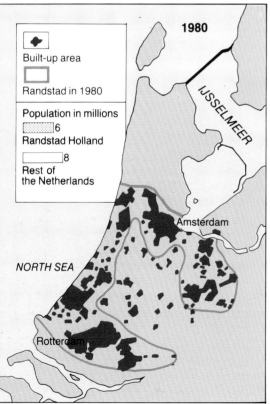

'God made the world but the Dutch made the Netherlands'. There is some truth in this old saying. For centuries, the Dutch have been reclaiming land from the sea to farm and to build on. The Netherlands is a small country with a very high population density – 344 people/km². Land is in short supply and there is much competition for it.

The west is the most crowded part of the Netherlands. The land is more fertile here than in the east. The population is concentrated in many towns and cities, which form a horseshoe shape. This is known as the Randstad or Ring City. Over 100 years ago, the towns were small. There were large areas of countryside between them. But in this century the towns have grown rapidly and much of the countryside has disappeared. This has happened because many people have moved from farms to new jobs in the towns. The four major cities are Rotterdam, The Hague, Amsterdam and Utrecht.

The population of the Netherlands has risen from 5.25 million in 1900, to over 14 million today. Not only are there many more people, but each person uses much more space. People today are wealthier than ever before. They spend much of their money on larger houses, cars, more travel and recreation, and more shopping. All these activities use up land.

Careful **land use planning** is very important when there is such great competition for space. Without it, much of the Greenheart – the area inside the Randstad – would now have been built over. This is an area of rich farmland. It is also important for recreation. There are many lakes which are used for sailing, fishing and other sports. The Greenheart's countryside can be reached quickly from the Randstad.

Because the Greenheart is so attractive, people have been moving from the cities to small towns and villages there. Businesses have moved into the region as well. Now there are daily flows of **commuters** from the countryside to the Randstad and from the Randstad to the countryside. But what has been done to prevent chaotic growth? The 'Third Report on Physical Planning in the Netherlands' was published in the mid-1970s. Some of its main proposals were:

(a) Build new housing in cities – people will, therefore, be less likely to move into the countryside.
(b) Accommodate people who do move out in special growth centres (picture 3).
(c) Create buffer zones to

1 Much of the Netherlands is either at or below sea level. Before strong sea defences were built, the risk of flooding was great. The occurrence of slightly higher ground in places largely explains the ring-shaped series of towns. In 1932 a dyke was built across the Ijsselmeer. Much land behind the dyke has been drained and is farmed. These lands are called 'polders'.

prevent neighbouring urban areas from joining up.

(d) Make stricter rules about building in rural areas – in many places this will not be allowed at all.

Change is going on around us all the time and it is important to plan it carefully. If mistakes are made now, it could be difficult and costly to put them right in the future.

1 How many times greater is population density in the Netherlands compared to Europe as a whole? (See page 9.)

2 Look at picture 1.
(a) How much of the Randstad was built up in 1900?
(b) How had it changed by 1980?
(c) What happened to the Greenheart between 1900 and 1980?

3 Make a copy of the 1980 map. With the help of an atlas, insert the names of the Randstad's other major cities.

4 (a) What percentage of the Netherlands' population lived in the Randstad in (i) 1900, (ii) 1980?
(b) In what ways do people use more space today than before?

5 Look at picture 2.
(a) How many buffer zones are there? What is their purpose?
(b) Where are the growth towns and growth centres?
(c) Why is the government planning for the future in this way?

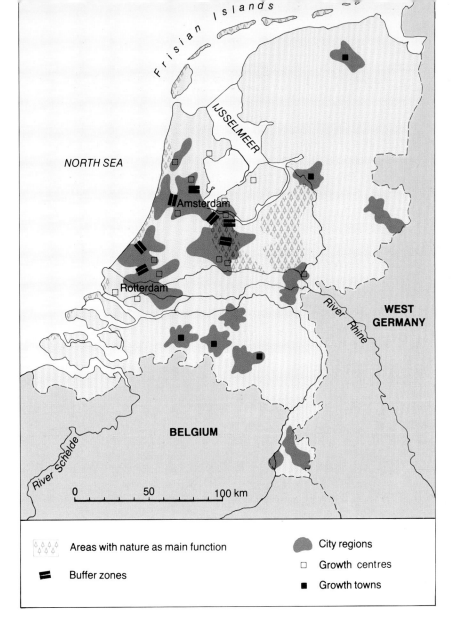

Key:
Areas with nature as main function

Buffer zones

City regions

Growth centres

Growth towns

2 (above) These are some of the proposals of the *Third Report on Physical Planning in the Netherlands*. At least 6000 new houses have to be built in ten years in growth centres and 10 000 in growth towns. The buffer zones will keep some countryside between the urban areas. Areas where nature comes first have also been set aside, according to this plan.

3 (below) New homes being built in the Randstad. Developments such as this are being controlled in order to keep the villages and farmland of the Greenheart unspoiled.

Difficult Environments

At Utsjoki the sun does not rise over the horizon between 26 November and 16 January. Moonlight is the only relief from midwinter darkness. This small town in the Finnish province of Lappland is 350 km inside the Arctic Circle. Life is hard in this frozen environment, where temperatures can fall to −45 °C.

Much has been done, however, to overcome the harsh climate. The province's previous isolation has largely been conquered. Lappland now has 8000 km of tarmac roads. Snow ploughs are used to keep them open when snow storms occur. Airports at Ivalo and Rovaniemi provide rapid links with Helsinki, Finland's capital city, and

elsewhere. Railways and buses also operate the whole year round. Shops and other services function normally, and people living in very isolated areas are served by mobile shops.

With the government's encouragement, tourism has developed fast. Lappland now has more than 16 000 beds available for tourists. People take holidays here to enjoy a range of activities. These include slalom, cross-country skiing, and reindeer and motor-sled safaris. As facilities improve, more people visit this beautiful wilderness. Difficult environments can be overcome more easily today, but they can also be more easily spoilt.

Development and **conservation** must be carefully balanced.

Finland's neighbours have also spent much money in their Arctic lands. In Norway and Sweden, the mineral wealth of the Northlands has attracted considerable investment. Development in the Soviet Union has been closely linked to the growth of Arctic ports.

The challenge of nature has been met in other parts of Europe too. Modern technology has overcome the deep, hostile waters of the North Sea. The valuable reserves of oil and gas below have made the huge cost of drilling worthwhile. In the Alps, long tunnels have been

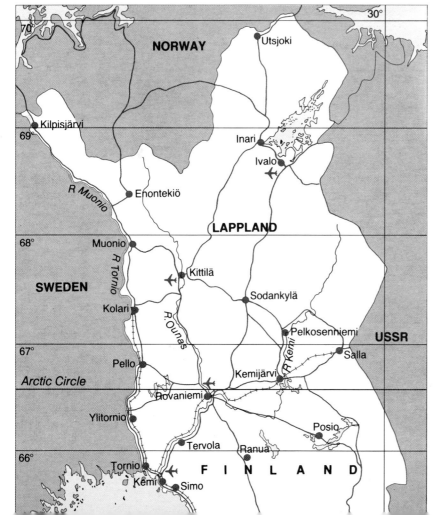

1 (left) Lappland is Finland's northern-most province. It is becoming more and more popular with tourists. They come for the wilderness, the Lapp culture and reindeer herdings, fishing, hiking and skiing. Most tourists enter through Rovaniemi, known as the gateway to Lappland. The biggest tourist centre in the wilds is Saariselkä. Use an atlas to find where this is situated in Lappland.

2 Lappland is Europe's largest continuous wilderness. The only signs of human activity over huge areas of land are the Lapps driving their motorized sleds.

blasted through hard rock. A tunnel, linking Britain and France, may soon be built under the English Channel. What new challenges will Europeans overcome in the future?

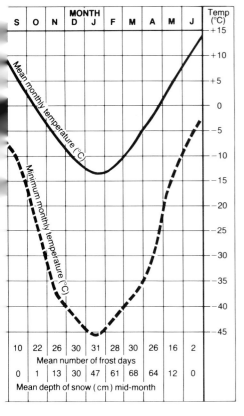

MONTH												Temp (°C)
S	O	N	D	J	F	M	A	M	J			

Mean monthly temperature (°C)

Minimum monthly temperature (°C)

10	22	26	30	31	28	30	26	16	2

Mean number of frost days

0	1	13	30	47	61	68	64	12	0

Mean depth of snow (cm) mid-month

3 Temperature, frost and snowfall in Lappland. Note how cold it can get in winter (−45 °C) and how deep its snow can be (68 cm).

1 (a) How many days of darkness does Utsjoki have in midwinter?
(b) Think about living in Utsjoki in midwinter darkness. What would your feelings be?
(c) How do you think you might spend your time in midwinter?

2 Look at picture 3.
(a) For each month write down the mean monthly temperature and the minimum monthly temperature.
(b) When is the difference greatest?
(c) Draw a line graph to show the mean number of frost days and the mean depth of snow for each month.

4 Thousands of people work on the North Sea's oil and gas platforms. Oil companies have to spend many millions of pounds to overcome this hostile environment.

3 How many other European countries have land inside the Arctic Circle?

4 How far is Utsjoki from (a) the airports at Ivalo and Rovaniemi, (b) Helsinki?

5 (a) Why is the government encouraging tourism in Lappland?
(b) Why do people want to holiday in this arctic region?
(c) Is it the type of place you would like to visit?
(d) Suggest some of the problems that a big increase in tourism could bring to Lappland.

6 (a) Why is it easier to overcome difficult environments today than it was in the past?
(b) Can you think of other examples of difficult environments that have been conquered, apart from those given on these pages?

5 The Alps are no longer such a great barrier to communication. Six major road tunnels speed the movement of goods and people between Northern Europe and Italy.

Acid Rain

Forests are dying. Fish have disappeared from thousands of lakes. Historic buildings are crumbling at a faster rate than ever before. The environment all over Europe is under attack from poison in the atmosphere.

Coal and oil-burning power stations, factories and motor vehicles constantly pump gases and particles into the air. The main **pollutants** from these sources are sulphur and nitrogen oxides. Unfortunately, what goes up must come down. This happens in two ways. The first is dry deposition – solid pollution that often falls quickly back to earth. The other form of pollution is acid rain. Here, the sulphur and nitrogen oxides in the atmosphere form weak sulphuric and nitric acids. These are held in the atmosphere and may travel thousands of kilometres, before falling with rain or snow.

Acid rain is an awful problem. As industry has grown, the atmosphere has become more polluted. Over 40 million tonnes of sulphur alone are poured into the atmosphere over Europe each year. This is having a devastating effect. In Sweden 4000 lakes are 'biologically dead' – the water is so acidic that no plant or fish can survive in it. In southern Norway, 80% of the lakes and streams are either dead, or in a critical condition.

1 This is what acid rain has done to forests in many parts of Europe.

Central Europe has been badly hit, too. Large areas of coniferous forest in Czechoslovakia, East Germany and West Germany are dead. Every country in Europe has been affected in some way.

Prevailing winds in Europe generally carry pollution from west to east. Britain causes the most air pollution in western Europe, but much of it falls on other countries. Britain has only just begun to reduce its pollution level. The technology exists to achieve lower levels of pollution but this costs money. The sulphur emitted from power stations can be reduced, but it means an increase in electricity bills. The necessary work on a

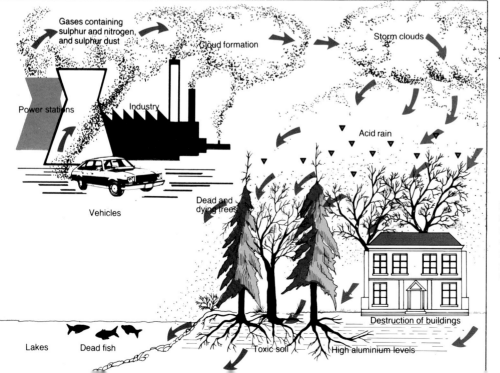

Gases containing sulphur and nitrogen, and sulphur dust

Cloud formation

Storm clouds

Power stations

Industry

Acid rain

Vehicles

Dead and dying trees

Destruction of buildings

Lakes

Dead fish

Toxic soil

High aluminium levels

2 Acid rain directly harms the areas it falls on. Also, as it passes through the soil, it reacts with metals such as aluminium and cadmium to form toxic substances. The rainwater washes these substances into rivers and lakes, where they gradually kill off the animals and plants in the water.

3 Rainfall is naturally acidic. Its acid content can be measured on the pH scale. This goes from 1 (most acidic) to 14 (most alkaline). A pH of 7 is neutral – neither acidic nor alkaline. Normal 'clean' rain has a pH of 5.6. Rain falling over most of Europe is much more acidic than this.

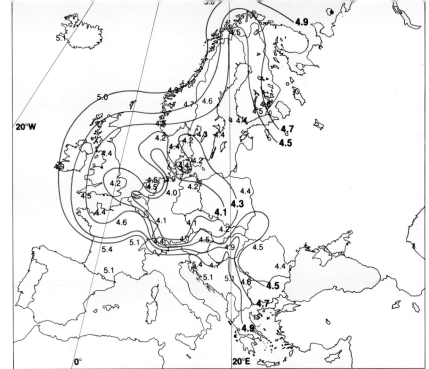

single power station could cost up to £150 million.

Most European countries have agreed to a 30% cut in emissions of sulphur dioxide from power stations and factories by 1993. Britain has decided to make some cuts in emissions but has not yet joined the '30% club'. This worries Britain's neighbours.

Since 1984, all fuels burned in Sweden must have a sulphur content of 1% or less. This will reduce acid rain, but Sweden really needs the help of other countries since 80% of the sulphur falling on the country comes from abroad.

4 (right) A 'dirty' picture postcard from Friends of the Earth.

5 (below) Many famous buildings in large cities are under attack from pollution. The amount of pollution is high because usually there is a lot of industry in and around cities. City traffic adds to the industrial pollution.

WE ♥ YOUR COUNTRY...
BUT NOT YOUR POLLUTION.
TO EUROPE

1 Look at picture 3.
(a) Where in Europe is rainfall most acidic and least acidic?
(b) Suggest reasons for these differences.

2 (a) What is the difference between 'dry deposition' and 'acid rain'?
(b) Make a list of the ways in which these two forms of pollution damage the environment.

3 Design a poster to make people more aware of the acid rain problem.

4 (a) Suggest ways in which Britain could reduce the pollution it causes.
(b) Try to find out what steps Britain has already taken to reduce the pollution its industry causes.
(c) Why has Britain not yet joined the '30% club'?

The Sewer of Europe?

Each year millions of people head for the Mediterranean's sun-drenched beaches. For many it is an escape from the noise and air pollution of their home towns. Yet parts of the Mediterranean Sea are so filthy that it has been tagged 'the sewer of Europe'. Richard Simmonds, a member of the European Parliament, has written: 'If you bathe, there's an odds-on chance of getting either throat complaints or some types of tummy trouble'. Nothing about this is in the holiday brochures!

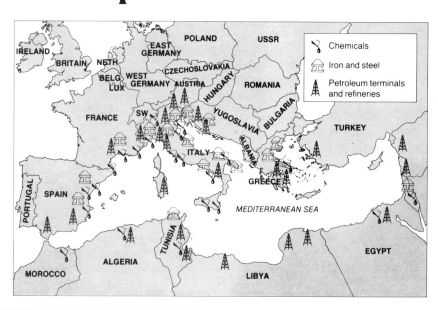

1 The coastline is a popular place for large factories. Heavy and bulky goods can be brought in and sent out by ship. The sea provides a plentiful supply of water for cooling systems. Firm, flat land is often found by the coast, and main roads and railways frequently follow coastlines. Labour is usually available, because many people live along the coast.

2 Factories are big polluters of the Mediterranean. However, because this pollution comes from a much smaller number of outlets than domestic sewage (which also pollutes the Mediterranean), it is easier to control if governments wish to do so. The law on pollution varies in its strictness from tough in France and Libya to non-existent in Morocco.

Much of the Mediterranean coastline is heavily populated. It is a popular place for people to live, and for factory sites. Increased tourism has led to even greater pressure on coastal land.

The simplest and cheapest way to get rid of the sewage of coastal towns is to dump it in the sea. This amounts to over 400 000 million tonnes a year. Most of it is untreated, and is often poured into the sea close

3 Oil pollution in Majorca. In many areas, sewage pollution is also a problem. The number of tourists visiting during the summer months produces more waste than the sewage system can handle. The problem is that most sewage systems have been designed only for the needs of the local people.

to popular beaches. But this is only part of the story. Factories sited along the coast pump all sorts of metals and chemicals into the sea. Pesticides and other chemicals from farms are disposed of in the same way. To add to this, one quarter of all the world's oil that is carried by tankers crosses the Mediterranean Sea. Oil gets into the water from small spillages and tanker collisions. It is also leaked by tankers washing their tanks illegally at sea. Rivers draining into the sea bring pollution from even further inland.

While all the waste poured into the sea is not harmful, the overall situation is serious. In 1976, all the Mediterranean countries (except Albania) signed the Barcelona Convention. They agreed to take steps to tackle pollution. Some progress has been made, but it is a huge and costly problem to solve. A Regional Oil Combating Centre has been set up in Malta to limit the damage from oil accidents. It provides equipment and experts at a moment's notice when a tanker spills oil.

Some popular tourist resorts are now spending money on treating sewage and building pipelines to carry it much further out to sea. Little is being done elsewhere, however. If this continues, what will the Mediterranean be like in 20 years time?

1 List the European and non-European countries which border the Mediterranean Sea?

2 On an outline map of the Mediterranean insert the major cities situated along the coastline, and the main rivers draining into the sea.

3 Using the map drawn for question 2 and picture 1, suggest which are the most heavily polluted areas of the sea.

4 Look at a selection of holiday brochures.
(a) On an outline map, mark all the places where holidays are advertised.
(b) What do the brochures say about the Mediterranean Sea?

5 List the European countries which do not have a coastline.

6 **Project idea:** Select a river, canal or stretch of coastline near to your school.
(a) Find out from the authority responsible (i) the extent of pollution, (ii) what has been done to reduce pollution.
(b) What evidence of pollution can you see yourself?
(c) Mount a class exhibition to promote the cleaning up of rivers, canals and the sea.

National Parks under Pressure

The managers of France's six national parks have problems. An increasing number of visitors has led to damaged vegetation, eroded footpaths and disturbed wildlife. On bank holidays, the car parks are often full and the most spectacular sites are crowded. Park managers have the difficult job of conserving the wildlife and landscapes of the parks while still offering people access to the countryside. The two aims can only be combined through careful management.

France's first national park, La Vanoise, was established in 1963. It is a high mountain park in the French Alps which has many peaks over 3000 m high. La Vanoise was set up to protect the last of the alpine wild goats, to bring town-dwellers into contact with mountain life, to promote rambling and skiing and to preserve the alpine scenery. The park itself covers 528 km². Nobody lives there and visitors have to obey special rules. Hunting, shooting and building are not allowed. The picking of fruit and flowers,

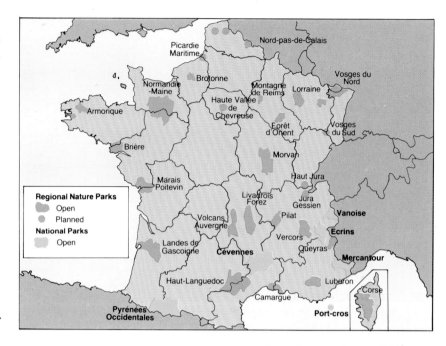

1 This shows the location of national parks and regional nature parks. Port-Cros is different from the other national parks. It is an island of only 694 ha, which has about 20 permanent inhabitants. The waters around the park are also protected up to a distance of 600 m. Because of the growing number of tourists wanting to visit this beautiful island, its preservation is now extremely difficult.

2 The six national parks vary in size, landscape and wildlife. However, they do have some things in common. All, except Port-Cros (a small island park), have a zone which runs round the park itself. This peripheral zone provides services to tourists. It reduces the damage to the park and helps to preserve its natural state and beauty.

camping, dogs, noise and litter are also banned.

Around the park is a 1465 km² peripheral zone where 13 700 people live – this area serves the park by providing facilities such as hotels and camping sites. Many of the people who live in the peripheral zone have jobs in tourism. Inside most national parks, areas called 'integrated reserves' can be cordoned off. These reserves have stricter rules which give extra protection to wildlife and vegetation. La Vanoise does not have any integrated reserves at present, but this may change as the number of visitors continues to rise.

As well as the national parks, there are 23 regional nature parks which are scattered throughout France. Here, the rules are not so strict because many more people live in these

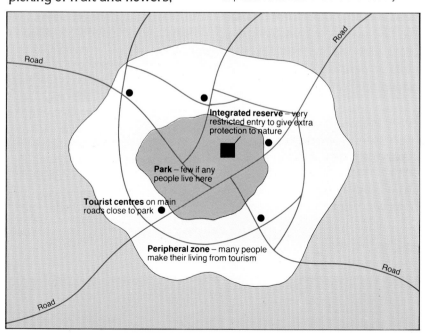

areas. Regional nature parks cater for the recreational need of city-dwellers, but also help to develop an understanding of nature and the environment. Like the national parks, they have their own wardens.

On a smaller scale again are the nature reserves. These are intended to protect unique plant and animal species, which are under threat because of the effects of modern life. They are spread widely throughout France. Most other countries protect the natural environment in similar ways. Without such careful management, many species of wildlife would become extinct and beautiful landscapes would be completely destroyed.

3 (above) Every year thousands of people choose a skiing holiday in La Vanoise National Park.

4 (left) Alpine wild goats live in La Vanoise National Park.

1 (a) Would you like to visit La Vanoise National Park? Give reasons for your answer.
(b) What is the main problem the park manager has to deal with?

2 Look at picture 1.
(a) With the help of an atlas, describe the location of the six national parks.
(b) Suggest why they are not more evenly spread around France.

3 (a) What are the main differences between national parks and regional nature parks?
(b) Describe how the regional nature parks are spread out around France.

4 (a) List ways in which people spoil the countryside.
(b) Now suggest ways in which the countryside could be improved.

5 Imagine you live in Paris and you want to visit La Vanoise. Use an atlas to describe the route you would take by car.

6 Why are many people who live in the peripheral zone of the park happy about the increase of tourism? Are there any disadvantages?

7 (a) Where is the nearest British national park to your school?
(b) What route would you take to get there?
(c) What attracts people to this national park?

Paris: the Inner City

Paris is one of the world's great cities. Every year millions of people visit famous landmarks such as the Eiffel Tower, the Champs Elysées and the Louvre. But few tourists are aware of the great problems Paris has. Yet its major difficulties are in the inner city, not far from the popular tourist attractions.

From Roman times, Paris has spread outwards to cover a huge area. Today, the historic City of Paris only forms the inner part of this built-up region. But here can be found all the problems of Europe's inner cities. Inner Paris suffers from great congestion of people, jobs and traffic. Housing is tightly packed. Much of it is poor in quality, and many homes are still without baths and inside toilets. Conditions are worst in the East End, traditionally the home of the Paris poor. The average population density in inner Paris is 207 people/ha. This compares with 78 people/ha in inner London. According to every measure, inner Paris is worse off than its outer suburbs. There is greater poverty, unemployment, crime and illness. Air pollution and noise are also higher.

Employment is concentrated in central Paris. Each day, over three-quarters of a million people travel from the suburbs to work. This puts a great strain on the transport system. Both the roads and the Metro (underground railway) are overcrowded. However, many inner city jobs in manufacturing have been lost in the last 20 years. Factories have closed because there is hardly any room to expand. Congestion on the roads also increases transport costs, and rates are high in the inner city.

It is not surprising, therefore, that the population of the inner city is falling. In 1921 it reached an all time high of 2.91 million. It has declined ever since. By 1982 it was down to 2.17 million. Most of the people who have moved out have gone to the outer suburbs. They feel this is a more pleasant place to live. A similar movement of people from inner to outer city has occurred in most other large European cities too.

Can inner city problems be solved? There is no doubt that this would be a difficult and expensive task. Paris, like other cities, has demolished many areas of old housing. These have been replaced by large blocks of council flats. But these are not always popular with the people who have to live in them. Recently, more money has been spent on **renovation**. Old buildings are brought up to modern standards by improving them, rather than by knocking them down and rebuilding. In this way long-established communities can be preserved.

1 The city of Paris and its suburbs.

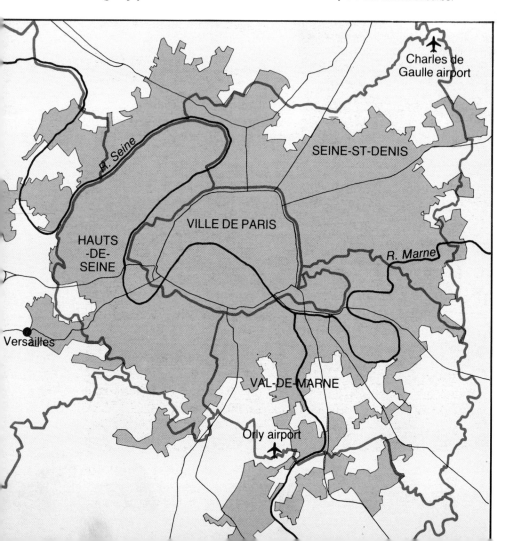

2 (above) New houses have been built in Paris where old, decaying property once stood. People have often found life unpleasant in these new developments. Many of them are badly designed and built.

3 (below) Many of the factories found in inner Paris have moved out or closed down. The result is fewer jobs for the people who still live there, and empty, decaying factory buildings.

1 How many times greater is the population density in inner Paris compared to inner London?

2 (a) Why do you think so many tower blocks were built in European cities in the 1960s and 1970s in an attempt to solve housing problems?
(b) What are the disadvantages of this type of housing?
(c) Why do many residents think it is better to renovate old housing?

3 The disadvantages of living in the inner city are well known. But many people think that inner city living has advantages too. Write about as many as you can.

4 (a) Why is there such a great concentration of jobs in the centre of Paris?
(b) List the jobs you would expect to find there.
(c) What problems does this create?

5 In what ways do suburban areas generally differ from inner cities?

4 Very poor housing conditions exist in parts of Paris, just as they do in many other major cities of Europe.

Holiday Europe

Every summer millions of Russians travel south to the Crimean coast. This is the USSR's riviera – the most popular holiday spot in the country. The annual holiday is an important break from work. People look forward to it all year.

Article 41 of the Soviet constitution states that 'every citizen has the right to a rest'. Workers have a minimum of 24 days off a year. Holidays are mainly organized by trade unions. Husbands and wives often take separate holidays because if they do not work in the same place it is likely they will be offered different holidays. There is little accommodation for children. They usually go to summer camps. So it is unusual to see a whole family on holiday together.

Holidays in the USSR are cheap. They are subsidized by the government. However, only 50 million places are available each year – not nearly enough for all the people that want them. Some of the unlucky ones make their own arrangements, but this can be very expensive.

Europe dominates the world of tourism (picture 2). At one time, most people took holidays in their own country. Now more and more people travel abroad, even to other continents. There are three main reasons for this trend. Annual holidays are longer than they used to be. Modern transport can take people long distances in a short time. People

also have more money to spend on luxuries such as holidays.

Tourism is a major industry in a number of countries. In Spain, the most popular destination for British holidaymakers, it is the main source of income. But while tourism brings in much money and provides many jobs, it also has disadvantages. Some of the most beautiful stretches of coastline are now heavily built-up. The most popular spots are often jammed with traffic. There is a limit to the pressure that the coastline can take. Of course, not everyone goes to the coast on

holiday. A growing number of people seek the attractions of historic cities such as Rome, Cologne and London. There are also many areas of countryside, particularly national parks, that have become very popular. As tourism increases, the need to plan carefully grows. It would be a pity if the most attractive parts of the continent became damaged beyond repair.

1 People travel long distances in the Soviet Union to holiday in the Black Sea resorts. Holiday towns are known as 'kurorts' – the German word for spas. In the Soviet Union many people see a holiday as a way of improving their health.

INTERNATIONAL TOURIST SPENDING millions US dollars				INTERNATIONAL TOURIST EARNINGS millions US dollars			
West Germany	15 236	Saudi Arabia	2 436	USA	10 632	Singapore	1 804
USA	11 697	Austria	2 130	Italy	7 823	Belgium/Lux	1 482
UK	6 010	Belgium/Lux	2 062	Spain	6 741	Netherlands	1 453
France	4 835	Sweden	1 819	France	6 560	Greece	1 448
Mexico	4 094	Australia	1 752	UK	5 243	Yugoslavia	1 432
Japan	3 882	Norway	1 647	West Germany	5 203	Australia	1 050
Canada	3 817	Italy	1 634	Mexico	5 057	Denmark	1 225
Netherlands	3 108	Denmark	1 251	Austria	4 724	Tonga	1 025
Venezuela	2 751	Kuwait	1 230	Switzerland	3 763	Sri Lanka	978
Switzerland	2 635	Spain	955	Canada	2 842	Sweden	963

2 (above) A list of the major countries involved in tourism. The number of people travelling abroad for a holiday is growing steadily. For many countries, tourism is a major source of income. The Soviet Union is not in either list. Few Russians travel abroad, and not many foreigners go to the Soviet Union for their holidays.

3 (left) Much building has taken place along the popular Black Sea coast in recent years. This type of development happened much earlier in many other places along western Europe's coastline.

1 (a) On an outline map of the world, use bars to show the information in picture 2.
(b) How many countries in each list are European?
(c) Which continent is not in either list? Suggest why.
(d) Calculate the difference between British tourist spending abroad and the amount spent by foreign tourists in Britain.
(e) Why does Britain want more foreign tourists to visit?

2 (a) Why do more people now go abroad for holidays than in the past?
(b) Suggest how tourism might change in the future.

3 (a) What do you think about the way holidays are arranged in the Soviet Union?
(b) Is tourism an important industry where you live?
(c) If it is, why do people visit the area.

(d) If it is not, is there any way that careful planning could attract tourists to the area in the future?

4 Ask everyone in the class where they would most like to go for a holiday in (a) Britain, (b) elsewhere in Europe. Collect all the results together and show them on outline maps. Try to use a different method to bars to display your results.

5 (a) What are the six most important things you want when choosing a holiday?
(b) Ask your parents the same question.
(c) If there are differences, try to explain why.

Europe Tomorrow

The year is 2010. Life in Europe has never been so good. Nobody is poor. Everyone has a job and decent housing. The average working week is 28 hours, spread over four days. People have more time and money to do what they want. The environment is much cleaner. Relations between the nations of eastern and western Europe are greatly improved. Much of the money that used to be spent on arms is now used to better the quality of life.

Is a Europe like this possible in the future? For it to happen, some of today's most difficult problems will have to be solved.

East and West
There has not been war in Europe for a long time. But every year more money is spent on weapons. Any war between NATO and the Warsaw Pact would cause great loss of life and damage. A nuclear war could lead to total destruction. Think of the benefits of cooperation rather than conflict.

Poverty
Europe is rich compared to Africa, Asia and South America. But millions of Europeans still live in poverty, and the gap between rich and poor is too big. Wealth will have to be shared more evenly within countries, if poverty is to end.

Unemployment and discrimination
In the last ten years, millions of people have lost their jobs. Ethnic minority groups have suffered most. But people are not only discriminated against because of race. It also occurs because of religion, culture, sex, age and physical handicap. Many peoples' lives have been spoiled by unemployment. Most west European governments say they cannot solve this huge problem now. Will they be able to do so in the future?

Housing
Europe has much housing which needs repair or replacement. The problem is worst in the inner cities. Here housing is usually older, poorer in quality and more overcrowded. Some people have no homes at all. Poor housing is a problem in rural areas too. It will take a great deal of money to put this right.

1 Arianne – Europe's own rocket. This gives West European scientists a greater chance of doing their own experiments in space, rather than relying on the US and the USSR. Building the Arianne has cost the 11 member nations of the European Space Agency $500 million.

Environment

Land, sea and air have been heavily polluted in many parts of Europe. Industrial wastes are not the only hazards, as the disaster in 1986 at the USSR's Chernobyl nuclear power station showed. This explosion poured dangerous radioactive particles all over Europe. We will have to be more careful about the way in which we use the environment. This is important for our own health and the wellbeing of future generations.

Can all these difficult problems be solved? It seems like a tall order. But change happens much more quickly than most people think.

2 A farmer in Alsace, France, checks cabbages for radiation levels following the disaster in 1986 at the USSR's Chernobyl nuclear reactor.

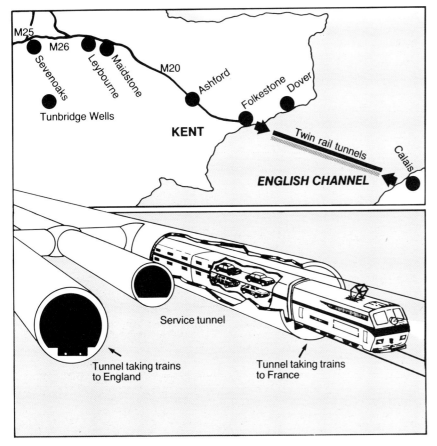

3 The proposed Channel Tunnel. There will be two tunnels, which will provide a rail link between Britain and France. Cars and other motor vehicles, including big trucks, will be carried on trains.

1 (a) How old will you be in 2010?
(b) Write a short essay explaining how you would like life to be then.

2 (a) Which of the five problems mentioned is the most important to solve? Explain why.
(b) Write about one other problem in Europe which has not been mentioned in this unit.
(c) Find out and discuss what others in the class have written about.

3 Ask some senior citizens how the world has changed since they were young. Do they think that it has changed for the better?

4 (a) Why do racial minority groups usually have a poorer standard of living than the average?
(b) In what other ways, apart from race, are people discriminated against?

5 **Project idea:** Find out what plans the council has for your local area in the future. These might affect housing, roads, shopping areas, parks, hospitals and schools.

Glossary

Assembly line: In assembly line work, a complicated job is broken down into many simpler tasks. Each task is done by a worker, group of workers, or robots, as the job moves from one work station to the next.

Balance of payments: The money a country earns from its *exports* minus the money it spends on *imports*.

Colonize: The settling and governing of a country or region by another country. The government of a colony is usually partly controlled by the home country.

Communism: The belief that all people should have equal opportunities in a classless society. Communist governments control nearly all industry, transport, education and health care.

Commuter: Someone who travels regularly to and from a place of work.

Conservation: The careful protection of the *environment* so that it is not destroyed.

Democracy: Government by leaders who have been elected by the people. Elections are held regularly and people can vote for different political parties.

Environment: Your surroundings at any particular time, such as where you live or work.

Exports: Goods that are produced in one country and sent to another to be sold. Services sold by one country to another also count as exports.

Ghetto: A densely populated district in a city where one particular group or nationality lives. It is often a very poor area.

Guaranteed prices: Prices which are held at a certain high level to protect an industry.

Guestworker: Someone who goes to another country to work, but does not enjoy the same rights as the citizens of that country.

Image: An idea or mental picture a person has of something, such as a place or another person.

Immigration: People moving into and settling down in a country where they were not born.

Imports: Goods that are brought in from another country. Services can also be imported.

Incentive: Benefit (usually grants of money or tax relief) given to companies to persuade them to set up factories or offices in a certain area. Incentives are sometimes given to individuals to encourage them to work harder.

Investment: Spending money on a project which it is believed will bring profits and other benefits (usually for a long time).

Land use planning: The careful planning of the way land is used to avoid spoiling the *environment*.

Manufacturing industries: Also known as secondary industries. These produce or manufacture things such as clothes, machines and food products from raw materials.

Minority: A group of people who are fewer in number than the main group(s). In Europe, blacks and Chinese are minority groups.

Multilateral disarmament: The giving up of nuclear weapons by all the countries of the world.

Multinational company: A company which has its headquarters in one country but produces goods in factories in at least one other country.

Neo-Nazi: Groups whose ideas are based on the Nazi party which controlled Germany from 1933 to 1945. These groups are violently opposed to racial and religious *minority* groups.

Neutral: A country which does not take sides in wars or disputes between other countries.

Pollutants: Waste products that are disposed of carelessly and dirty the air, water or land.

Population density: The average number of people living in a square kilometre. It can be worked out for any area – for example, a borough, a region or a country.

Primary industries: These consist of mining, farming, fishing and forestry. They provide raw materials and food.

Racism: The belief that people of certain racial origins are inferior.

Renovation: The repair and modernization of buildings which are out-of-date and in poor condition.

Service industries: Also known as tertiary industries. They provide a service of some kind – for example, the banking, transport and health services.

Standard of living: How well off and comfortable people are. People's standard of living depends on how much they have to spend on food, clothes, housing, lighting, heating, travel to work, entertainment and holidays. It also depends on whether they have good schools and colleges, proper medical care, social security, welfare services, water supplies, electricity, sewage disposal and good transport and communication systems.

Stereotype: A fixed view or *image* of groups of people, which suggests that they all share certain characteristics.

Superpower: The USA and USSR are superpowers. They have large populations, are rich in natural resources, and have the largest armies and greatest stocks of weapons in the world. They therefore have a lot of power over other smaller, poorer countries.

Trade bloc: Countries which group together to protect their trade interests – for example, Comecon.

Unilateral disarmament: The giving up of all nuclear weapons by one country, or group of countries, without regard to whether other countries are prepared to give them up.